English Communication I

English Communication I

발 행 | 2024년 03월 11일
저 자 | 김지현
펴낸이 | 한건희
펴낸곳 | 주식회사 부크크
출판사등록 | 2014.07.15.(제2014-16호)
주 소 | 서울특별시 금천구 가산디지털1로 119 SK트윈타워 A동 305호
전 화 | 1670-8316
이메일 | info@bookk.co.kr

ISBN | 979-11-410-7589-7

www.bookk.co.kr

English Communication I

김지현 지음

CONTENT

창신대학교 성인 학습자들에게 이 책을 바칩니다.

이 교재는 KOCW에 올려진 English Communication I을 학습할 때 함께 사용할 수 있도록 집필하였습니다. 성인 학습자의 일상생활과 밀접한 주제 중심으로 구성하였으며 어휘와 문법을 익히고, 듣고 말하기 연습을 하며, 읽고 쓰기 활동을 통해서 익힌 내용을 더 강화하여, 상황에 맞는 표현을 잘 선택하여 소통할 수 있는 능력을 배양하는 것에 중점을 두었습니다. 성인 학습자들이 English Communication I을 통하여 '영어 울렁증'을 극복할 수 있기를 바랍니다.

2024년 3월

저자 김지현

1 주차 1차시 학습:

For the First Time

Learning Objectives:

Introduce yourself and spell your name.

Say hello to someone you meet for the first time.

Vocabulary

A a	**N n**
B b	**O o**
C c	**P p**
D d	**Q q**
E e	**R r**
F f	**S s**
G g	**T t**
H h	**U u**
I i	**V v**
J j	**W w**
K k	**X x**
L l	**Y y**
M m	**Z z**

Pronunciation

Repeat after the teacher.

A a	N n
B b	O o
C c	P p
D d	Q q
E e	R r
F f	S s
G g	T t
H h	U u
I i	V v
J j	W w
K k	X x
L l	Y y
M m	Z z

Remember this!

B(b)와 P(b)를 발음할 때 유의할 점:

B(b): 아랫입술과 윗입술을 붙이고 성대를 울리면서 발음합니다. 손을 목에 대고 발음하였을 때, 성대가 울리는 것을 느낄 수 있으면 세내로 발음한 것입니다.

P(p): B(b)를 발음할 때의 입 모양을 유지하고 성대를 울리지 말고 편하게 발음합니다.

F(f)와 V(v)를 발음할 때 유의할 점:

F(f): 이 철자의 발음을 마무리할 때는 윗니를 아랫입술에 대면 됩니다.

V(v): 이 철자의 발음을 시작할 때는 F f의 발음을 마무리할 때와 같이 윗니를 아랫입술에 올리고 성대를 울리면서 발음하면 됩니다.

L(l)을 발음할 때 유의할 점:

이 철자의 발음을 마무리할 때는 혀끝을 입천장 앞쪽에 붙여주면 됩니다.

R(r)을 발음할 때 유의할 점:

입술을 약간 벌려서 앞쪽으로 내밀면서 성대를 울리며 발음하면 됩니다. 이때 '알'이라고 발음하지 말고 '아'라고 길게 발음하면 R r의 소리를 들을 수 있습니다.

Z(z)를 발음할 때 유의할 점:

S s의 발음을 마무리할 때의 입 모양을 하고 성대를 동시에 울려주며 발음하면 됩니다.

Everyday Expressions!

Asking for personal information

What's your name?

How do you spell that?

Giving personal information

My name's Chi-Hyun.

I'm Chi-Hyun.

It's Chi-Hyun.

Chi-Hyun.

My name's spelt C-H-I hyphen H-Y-U-N.

It's spelt C-H-I hyphen H-Y-U-N.

C-H-I hyphen H-Y-U-N.

Asking for personal information	Giving personal information
What's your name?	My name's Chi-Hyun.
	It's Chi-Hyun.
	I'm Chi-Hyun.
	Chi-Hyun.
How do you spell that?	My name's spelt C-H-I hyphen H-Y-U-N
	It's spelt C-H-I hyphen H-Y-U-N.
	C-H-I hyphen H-Y-U-N

Remember this!

회화할 때는 축약할 수 있는 부분은 다 축약하고 한 번 언급된 명사구는 대명사로 대신합니다.

1. **일반적으로 be-동사의 축약형을 사용합니다.** 예: "My name is Chi-Hyun."의 be-동사 is를 축약해서 's로 표현됩니다. 질문을 받지 않고 스스로 자기소개를 할 때도 아래의 문장을 사용하면 됩니다.

"My name's Chi-Hyun."

2. **한 번 언급된 명사구를 대명사로 표현합니다.** 예: "My name is Chi-Hyun."을 축약할 수 있는 부분은 주어인 my name입니다. 이름이 무엇이냐는 질문에 답을 할 때는 name이 한 번 언급되었으므로 이것을 대신할 수 있는 대명사는 it입니다. 그러므로 아래의 문장으로 표현할 수도 있습니다.

"It's Chi-Hyun."

3. **묻는 정보만 짧게 답을 할 수 있습니다.** 예: 이름이 무엇이냐는 질문을 받았을 때는 이름만 말하면 됩니다. 아래와 같이 말하면 됩니다.

"Chi-Hyun."

그러나 지인이 아닌 경우에는 완전한 문장으로 대화를 나누는 것이 좋습니다. 완전한 문장으로 말하는 것은 존댓말을 사용하는 것과 같습니다.

1 주차 2차시 학습:

For the First Time

Learning Objectives:

Introduce yourself and spell your name.

Say hello to someone you meet for the first time.

Pronunciation

Remember this!

이름의 철자를 불러줄 때는 한 글자씩 인토네이션을 잘 살려서 천천히 발음해야 합니다. 그렇지 않으면 상대방이 잘 못 알아들을 수 있습니다. KOCW에 업로드된 English Communication I 1주차 2차시의 동영상에서 발음하는 것처럼 해 보세요.

Repeat after the teacher.

<table>
<tr><th>Asking for personal information</th><th>Giving personal information</th></tr>
<tr><td rowspan="4">What's your name?</td><td>My name's Chi-Hyun.</td></tr>
<tr><td>It's Chi-Hyun.</td></tr>
<tr><td>I'm Chi-Hyun.</td></tr>
<tr><td>Chi-Hyun.</td></tr>
<tr><td rowspan="3">How do you spell that?</td><td>My name's spelt C-H-I hyphen H-Y-U-N</td></tr>
<tr><td>It's spelt C-H-I hyphen H-Y-U-N.</td></tr>
<tr><td>C-H-I hyphen H-Y-U-N</td></tr>
</table>

Speaking

Read the conversation with the teacher.

You:	**What's your name?**
Teacher:	**My name's Chi-Hyun.**
You:	**How do you spell that?**
Teacher:	**It's spelt C-H-I hyphen H-Y-U-N.**

Now, read the conversation again. This time, the teacher will use the other expressions under Everyday Expressions.

1.

You:	**What's your name?**
Teacher:	**It's Chi-Hyun.**
You:	**How do you spell that?**
Teacher:	**It's spelt C-H-I hyphen H-Y-U-N.**

2.

You:	**What's your name?**
Teacher:	**I'm Chi-Hyun.**
You:	**How do you spell that?**
Teacher:	**It's spelt C-H-I hyphen H-Y-U-N.**

3.

You:	**What's your name?**
Teacher:	**Chi-Hyun.**
You:	**How do you spell that?**
Teacher:	**C-H-I hyphen H-Y-U-N.**

Now it's your turn to answer the teacher's questions.

Teacher:	**What's your name?**
You:	________________
Teacher:	**How do you spell that?**
You:	________________

Everyday Expressions!

Saying hello for the first time

Hello!

Hi!

I'm Chi-Hyun.

My name's Chi-Hyun.

It's nice to meet you.

It's nice to meet you, too.

Nice to meet you.

Nice to meet you, too.

Pronunciation

Repeat after the teacher.

It's nice to meet you.

It's nice to meet you, too.

Nice to meet you.

Nice to meet you, too.

Speaking

Practice the conversation with the teacher.

1. Chi-Hyun: **Hi! I'm Chi-Hyun. What's your name?**
   Young-Chan: **Hi, Chi-Hyun. I'm Young-chan.**
   Chi-Hyun: **It's nice to meet you, Young-chan.**
   Young-Chan: **Nice to meet you, too.**

2. Chi-Hyun: **Hi! My name's Chi-Hyun. What's your name?**
   Young-Chan: **Hi, Chi-Hyun. I'm Young-chan.**
   Chi-Hyun: **Nice to meet you, Young-chan.**
   Young-Chan: **Nice to meet you, too.**

Now, it's your turn to say hello to the teacher.

1. Teacher: **Hi! I'm Chi-Hyun. What's your name?**
   You: ______________________________
   Teacher:: **It's nice to meet you, Young-chan.**
   You: ______________________________

이번에는 아래의 내용에 여러분의 이름을 사용해서 대화에 참여하면 됩니다.

Teacher: **Hi! I'm Chi-Hyun. What's your name?**
You: **Hi, Chi-Hyun. I'm _______. (My name's_____.)**
Teacher: **Nice to meet you.**
You: **Nice to meet you, too. (It's nice to meet you, too.)**

2. You: ______________________

Teacher: **Hi, I'm Chi-Hyun.**

You: ______________________

Teacher: **Nice to meet you, too.**

이번에는 여러분이 대화를 시작하세요. 아래의 대화문에 여러분의 이름을 사용해서 참여하면 됩니다.

You: **Hi, I'm ____________. (What's your name?)**

Teacher: **Hi, I'm Chi-Hyun.**

You: **It's nice to meet you. (Nice to meet you.)**

Teacher: **Nice to meet you, too.**

Remember this!

영어권 나라에서는 이름을 불러주며 인사합니다. 그러므로 처음 만났지만 계속 마주칠 것 같은 사람들일 경우에는 인사할 때 이름을 알려 줍니다. 그래서 What's your name? 이라는 질문을 받지 않아도 인사와 함께 이름을 말합니다. 상대방이 이름을 알려 주며 인사할 때는 여러분의 이름도 알려 줘야 합니다. 만약에 여러분이 이름을 알려 주는 것을 잊어버렸다면 상대방이 여러분의 이름을 물어볼 것입니다. 그때 알려 주어도 됩니다. 알려 주는 이름을 잘 듣고 이름을 불러주면서 인사를 하면 상대방에게 좋은 인상을 남길 것입니다. 그리고 이름을 기억해서 다시 만날 때 불러주면 더 좋습니다.

What can you do now?

	Yes, I can.	Mostly yes.	Not yet.
I can introduce myself and spell my name.			
I can say hello to someone I meet for the first time.			

2 주차 1차시 학습:

Personal Information

Learning Objectives:

Say phone numbers and email addresses.

Ask someone to repeat something or spell something.

Review

I. Complete the conversations.

1. **A:** ____________________

B: **I'm Young-Chan.**

a. Whats your name?
b. How do you spell that?

2. **A:** ____________________________

B: **It's spelt Y-O-U-N-G hyphen C-H-A-N.**

a. Whats your name?
b. How do you spell that?

II. Choose all the sentences that can be used to answer the question.

1. **A:** **What's your name?**

B: ____________________

a. I'm Young-Chan.
b. It's Young-Chan.
c. Y-O-U-N-G hyphen C-H-A-N
d. Young-Chan.

2. **A:** **How do you spell that?**

B: ____________________

a. Y-O-U-N-G hyphen C-H-A-N
b. It's spelt Y-O-U-N-G hyphen C-H-A-N
c. My names spelt Y-O-U-N-G hyphen C-H-A-N. Chan is spelt with capital C.
d. Young-Chan.

III. Complete the conversation.

A:	**Hi. I'm Young-Chan.**
B:	____________________
A:	**Nice to meet you.**
B:	**Nice to meet you.**

a. Hi, Young-Chan. I'm Carol.
b. What's your name?
c. Hi. My name's Young-Chan.
d. Nice to meet you, too.

Vocabulary

0	**zero**	5	**five**	@	**at**
1	**one**	6	**six**	.com	**dot com**
2	**two**	7	**seven**	.net	**dot net**
3	**three**	8	**eight**	.edu	**dot E-D-U**
4	**four**	9	**nine**		

Pronunciation

Repeat after the teacher.

0	**zero**	5	**five**	@	**at**
1	**one**	6	**six**	.com	**dot com**
2	**two**	7	**seven**	.net	**dot net**
3	**three**	8	**eight**	.edu	**dot E-D-U**
4	**four**	9	**nine**		

Everyday Expressions!

Asking for personal information

What's your **name**?

What's your **email address**?

What's your **phone number**?

Giving personal information

My **email address** is carolk@cs.ac.kr.

It's carolk@cs.ac.kr.

carolk@cs.ac.kr.

My **phone number** is 055-250-1297.

It's 055-250-1297.

055-250-1297.

Asking for personal information	Giving personal information
What's your email address?	**My email address is carolk@cs.ac.kr.**
	It's carolk@cs.ac.kr.
	carolk@cs.ac.kr.
What's your phone number?	**My phone number is 055-250-1207.**
	It's 055-250-1297.
	055-250-1297.

Pronunciation

Repeat after the teacher.

<table>
<tr><th>Asking for personal information</th><th>Giving personal information</th></tr>
<tr><td rowspan="3">What's your email address?</td><td>My email address is carolk@cs.ac.kr.</td></tr>
<tr><td>It's carolk@cs.ac.kr.</td></tr>
<tr><td>carolk@cs.ac.kr.</td></tr>
<tr><td rowspan="3">What's your phone number?</td><td>My phone number is 055-250-1207.</td></tr>
<tr><td>It's 055-250-1297.</td></tr>
<tr><td>055-250-1297.</td></tr>
</table>

2 주차 2차시 학습:

Personal Information

Learning Objectives:

Say phone numbers and email addresses.

Ask someone to repeat something or spell something.

Grammar

<table>
<tr><th colspan="6">Subject Pronouns</th></tr>
<tr><td>I am
I'm</td><td rowspan="4">a student</td><td>You are
You're</td><td rowspan="4">students.</td><td rowspan="2">It is
It's</td><td rowspan="2">a pen.</td></tr>
<tr><td>You are
You're</td><td rowspan="2">We are
We're</td></tr>
<tr><td>He is
He's</td><td rowspan="2">They are
They're</td><td rowspan="2">pens.</td></tr>
<tr><td>She is
She's</td><td>They are
They're</td></tr>
</table>

Remember this!

- 주어로 사용하는 단수형 대명사: **I, You(너), He, She, It**
- 주어로 사용하는 복수형 대명사: **You(여러분), We, They**

Possessive Adjectives			
My	name	is ('s)	Chi-Hyun
Your			Young-hee.
His			Young-chan.
Her			Mi-ok.
Your	numbers	are	3 and 4.
Our			5 and 6.
Their			7 and 8.
Its	name	is ('s)	Bokdori.
Their	names	are	Bokdori and Boksooni.

Remember this!

•소유격 대명사(possessive adjectives)는 명사구 앞에서 명사구를 꾸며줍니다.

Let's check how much you understand!

Complete the sentences. Use contractions whenever possible.

1. I*'m*__ Young-Hee. I*'m*__ a student.

2. My name ____ Young-Hee.

3. Young-Chan: **What's your name?**

Young-Hee: **It____ Young-Hee.**

4. We____ students.

5. Our professor____ Chi-Hyun Kim.

6. He____ a student, too.

7. Their professor____ Adam Smith.

Pronunciation

Repeat after the teacher.

I'm a student.

You're a student.

She's a student.

He's a student.

You're students.

We're students.

They're students.

It's a pen.

They're pens.

> ***Remember this!***
>
> 회화할 때는 위와 같이 대명사를 주어로 사용하는 문장은 be 동사를 축약해서 발음합니다.

Pronunciation

Repeat after the teacher.

Your numbers are 3 and 4.

Our numbers are 5 and 6.

Their numbers are 7 and 8.

My name's Chi-Hyun.

Your name's Young-Hee.

His name's Young-Chan.

Her name's Mi-Ok.

Its name's Bokdori.

Their names are Bokdori and Boksooni.

Remember this!

회화할 때는 위와 같이 소유격 형용사를 사용하는 명사구를 주어로 사용하는 문장은 be-동사 is만 축약해서 발음합니다.

Listening

What do you hear? Choose the words you hear form the box

you're	your	they're	their

1. ______

2. ______

3. ______ ______

4. ______

5. ______

You should have heard these sentences.

1. What's **your** name?
2. **Their** names are Young-Hee and Young-Chan.
3. **They're** **your** students.
4. What are **their** names?
5. **You're** students.

Everyday Expressions!

Asking someone to repeat something

Could you repeat that, please?

Asking someone to spell something

How do you spell that?

Could you spell that, please?

Speaking

Practice the conversation with thte teacher.

You: **What's your email address?**

Teacher: **It's carolk at C-S dot A-C dot K-R.**

You: **Could you spell carolk, please?**

Teacher: **(Sure.) C-A-R-O-L-K.**

You: **Thanks. Could you repeat your email address?**

Teacher: **(Sure.) It's carolk at C-S dot A-C dot K-R.**

You: **Thank you. And your phone number?**

Teacher: **It's oh-five-five-two-five-oh-one-two-nine-seven.**

You: **Could you repeat that, please?**

Teacher: **It's oh-five-five-two-five-oh-one-two-nine-seven.**

You: **Thanks.**

Teacher: **You're welcome**

Remember this!

위의 대화문에서 사용된 질문 중에 And your phone number?는 What's your phone number?를 줄여서 표현한 것입니다. 이렇게 줄인 표현을 사용할 수 있는 이유는 대화문의 첫 질문(What's your email address?)과 같은 유형의 질문이어서 문장을 줄여서 표현할 수 있는 것입니다.

Now write in your own information to complete the conversation. Then answer the teacher's questions.

Teacher: **What's your email address?**

You: ______________________ ________

Teacher: **Could you spell that, please?**

You: ______________________________

Teacher: **Thanks. Could you repeat your email address?**

You: ______________________________

Teacher: **Thank you. And your phone number?**

You: ______________________________

Teacher: **Could you repeat that, please?**

You: ______________________________

Teacher: **Thanks.**

You: **You're welcome.**

What can you do now?

	Yes, I can.	Mostly yes.	Not yet.
I can say my phone number and email address.			
I can ask someone to repeat something or spell something.			

3 주차 1차시 학습:

Favorite Things

Learning Objectives:

Talk about your favorite things.

Ask about personal interests.

Review

I. Complete the conversations.

1. **A:** ____________________

B: **It's carolk@cs.ac.kr.**

a. What's your phone number?

b. What's your email address?

2. **A:** ____________________

B: **It's 055-250-1297.**

a. What's your phone number?

b. What's your email address?

II. Choose all the sentences that can be used to answer the question.

A: **What's your email address?**

B: ____________________

a. My email address is carolk@cs.ac.kr.

b. It's carolk@cs.ac.kr.

c. carolk@cs.ac.kr.

d. carolk.

III. Say the email address below.

carolk@naver.com

IV. Say the phone number below.

055-250-1141

V. What sentences can you use to complete the conversation? Find the sentences.

A:	**What's your name?**
B:	**It's Soo-Young.**
A:	______________
B:	**S-O-O hyphen Y-O-U-N-G.**
A:	**Thank you.**

a. What's your phone number?
b. Could you spell that?
c. What's your email address?
d. How do you spell that?

VI. What sentences can you use to complete the conversation? Find the sentences.

A:	**What's your phone number?**
B:	**It's 055-250-1297.**
A:	______________
B:	**055-250-1297.**
A;	**Thank you.**

a. Could you repeat that, please?
b. Could you spell that, please?
c. What's your email address?
d. How do you spell that, please?

VII. Fill in the blanks with the words in the box.

my	your	her	his
its	their	our	your
I'm	you're	she's	he's
it's	they're	we're	you're

1. ________ Young-Hee. My phone number is 055-264-1141.

2. My pets are dogs. ________ names are Bokdori and Boksooni.

3. We're students. ________ English professor is Chi-Hyun Kim.

4. Young-Chan is a student, and ________ friend is a student, too.

5. Young-Hee and Chul-Soo are students. ________ in class, now.

Vocabulary

trot	트로트
classical music	클래식 음악
a pop ballad (pop ballads)	발라드
a singer (singers)	가수
an idol group (idol groups)	아이돌 그룹
a boy band/group (boy ands/groups)	남성 밴드
a girl band/group (girl bands/groups)	여성 밴드
popular	인기있는
favorite	가장 좋아하는
my favorite (my favorites)	내가 가장 좋아하는 것

a sport (sports)	스포츠
baseball	야구
a baseball player (baseball players)	야구선수
a baseball team (baseball teams)	야구팀
basketball	농구
a basketball player (basketball players)	농구선수
a basketball team (basketball teams)	농구팀
soccer	축구
a soccer player (soccer players)	축구선수
a soccer team (soccer teams)	축구팀

Pronunciation

Repeat after the teacher.

My favorite kind of music is **classical music**.

That's **trot**. (This is **trot**.)

Lee Moon Sae is a **ballad singer**.

BTS is a K-pop **boy band**.

BLACKPINK is a **girl group**.

My **favorite sport** is soccer.

My **favorite soccer player** is Heung-Min Son.

My **favorite soccer team** is Manchester United.

Remember this!

This vs That

This와 That은 사물의 위치 기준으로 사물의 정체를 알려 줄 때만 사용하는 것이 아니라 소리의 위치 기준으로 소리의 정체를 알려 줄 때도 사용합니다.

예:
가까이서 들리거나 바로 앞에서 들리는 소리의 정체를 설명할 때:

This is trot. 이것은 트로트입니다
This is Lee Moon Sae. 이것은 이문세의 노래입니다.

멀리서 들리는 소리의 정체를 설명할 때:

That's trot. 저것은 트로트입니다.
That's Lee Moon Sae. 저 노래는 이문세의 노래입니다.

Everyday Expressions!

Asking about personal interests
What are you interested in?

Talking about your favorite things
I'm into trot now.
I'm into ballads now.
I'm into Pilates.

I'm interested in sports. My favorite sport is soccer.

Pronunciation

Repeat after the teacher.

Asking about favorite things	Talking about your favorite things
What are you interested in?	I'm into trot now.
	I'm into ballads now.
	I'm into Pilates now.
	I'm interested in sports. My favorite is soccer.

3 주차 2차시 학습:

Favorite Things

Learning Objectives:

Talk about your favorite things.

Ask about personal interests.

Grammar

Yes/No Questions		Short Answers	
Is it	your favorite?	Yes, it is.	No, it's not. (No, it isn't.)
Are they	your favorites?	Yes, they are.	No, they're not. (No, they aren't.)

Yes/No Questions		Short Answers	
Are you	students?	Yes, we are.	No, we're not. (No, we aren't)
Are they		Yes, they are.	No, they're not. (No, they aren't.)

Yes/No Questions		Short Answers	
Are you	a student?	Yes, I am.	No, I'm not.
Is he		Yes, he is.	No, he's not. (No, he isn't.)
Is she		Yes, she is.	No, she's not. (No, she isn't.)

Let's check how much you understand!

Complete the sentences.

1. A: **Are you a student?**

B: **Yes,** *I am* ________.

2. A: **Are Chul-Soo and Chi-Hyun students?**

B: **No,** ________________.

3. A: **Is Young-Hee a student?**

B: **Yes,** ________________.

4. A: **Is Chul-Soo a student?**

B: **No,** ________________.

5. A: **Is it your favorite?**

B: **Yes,** ________________.

Pronunciation

Repeat after the teacher.

<table>
<tr><th colspan="2">Yes/No Questions</th><th colspan="2">Short Answers</th></tr>
<tr><td>Are you</td><td rowspan="3">a student?</td><td>Yes, I am.</td><td>No, I'm not.</td></tr>
<tr><td>Is he</td><td>Yes, he is.</td><td>No, he's not.
(No, he isn't.)</td></tr>
<tr><td>Is she</td><td>Yes, she is.</td><td>No, she's not.
(No, she isn't.)</td></tr>
</table>

<table>
<tr><th colspan="2">Yes/No Questions</th><th colspan="2">Short Answers</th></tr>
<tr><td>Are you</td><td rowspan="2">students?</td><td>Yes, we are.</td><td>No, we're not.
(No, we aren't)</td></tr>
<tr><td>Are they</td><td>Yes, they are.</td><td>No, they're not.
(No, they aren't.)</td></tr>
</table>

<table>
<tr><th colspan="2">Yes/No Questions</th><th colspan="2">Short Answers</th></tr>
<tr><td>Is it</td><td>your favorite?</td><td>Yes, it is.</td><td>No, it's not.
(No, it isn't.)</td></tr>
<tr><td>Are they</td><td>your favorites?</td><td>Yes, they are.</td><td>No, they're not.
(No, they aren't.)</td></tr>
</table>

Listening

What do you hear? Choose the words you hear from the box.

you	he	she	they	it

1. ____ **1.** Is ____ your car?

2. ____ **2.** Is ____ your friend?

3. ____ **3.** Is ____ your friend?

4. ____ **4.** Are ____ a student?

5. ____ **5.** Are ____ students?

Speaking

Check if the information is correct. Practice speaking with the teacher.

1. That is trot.

You: *Is that trot?*

Teacher. Yes, *it is.*

2. This is trot.

You: ______________________________

Teacher: **No,** ______________________________

3. Lee Moon Sae is a ballad singer.

You: ______________________________

Teacher: **Yes,** ______________________________

4. BTS is a K-pop boy band.

You: ______________________________

Teacher: **Yes,** ______________________________

5. BLACKPINK is a girl group.

You: ______________________________

Teacher: **Yes,** ______________________________

6. My favorite kind of music is classical music.

You: ______________________________

Teacher: **Yes,** ______________________________

7. Classical music is my favorite kind of music.

You: ______________________________

Teacher: **Yes,** ______________________________

8. My favorite sport is soccer.

You: ______________________________

Teacher: **Yes,** ______________________________

9. Soccer is my favorite sport.

You: ______________________________

Teacher: **Yes,** ______________________________

10. My favorite soccer player is Heung-Min Son.

You: ______________________________

Teacher: **Yes,** ______________________________

11. Heung-Min Son is my favorite soccer player.

You: ______________________________

Teacher: **Yes,** ______________________________

12. My favorite soccer team is Manchester United.

You: ______________________________

Teacher: **Yes,** ______________________________

13. Manchester United is my favorite soccer team.

You: ____________________

Teacher: **Yes,** ____________________

What can you do now?

	Yes, I can	Mostly yes.	Not yet.
I can talk about my favorite things.			
I can ask about personal interests			

4 주차 1차시 학습:

Countries and Nationalities

Learning Objectives:

Name countries and nationalities.

Ask where someone is from.

Ask where someone or something is.

Review

I. Fill in the blanks with *'m*, *is*, or *are*..

1. The NC Dinos ______ my favorite baseball team.

2. BTS and BLACKPINK ____ K-pop groups.

3. I _____ into games.

4. Our favorite kind of music ____ trot.

5. Their favorite ____ soccer.

II. Choose all the sentences that can be used to answer the question.

A: What are you interested in?

B: ____________________________

a. I'm interested in trot.
b. Trot is popular.
c. My favorite is trot.
d. I'm into trot.

III. Check the correct sentences.

1. ( ) I'm into a ballad.

2. ( ) I'm into ballads.

3. ( ) I'm into ballad.

Remember this!

음악 장르가 셀 수 있는 명사와 셀 수 없는 명사로 표현됩니다.

countable	uncountable
a ballad (ballads)	trot
	classical music
	hip hop
	rap
	pop music

항상 변치 않는 사실을 전달 할 때, 그 사실이 셀 수 있는 명사와 관련된 것이라면 그 명사는 복수형으로 표현되어야 합니다.

예: I'm into **computers**. 컴퓨터에 관심이 있습니다.
(computer는 셀 수 있는 명사입니다.)

I'm into **games**. 게임에 관심이 있습니다.
(game은 셀 수 있는 명사입니다.)

I'm into **soccer**. 축구에 관심이 있습니다.
(soccer는 셀 수 없는 명사입니다.)

I'm into **science**.
(science는 셀 수 없는 명사입니다.)

IV. Check the correct sentences.

1. (   ) I'm soccer.

2. (   ) My favorite is soccer.

3. (   ) My favorite sport is soccer.

V. Check the correct sentences.

1. (   ) Are you a student?

2. (   ) Are you student?

3. (   ) Are you students?

VI. Check the correct sentences.

1. (   ) That's a ballad.

2. (   ) That's a trot.

3. (   ) That's trot.

VII. Complete the conversations.

1. A: **Are they students?**

B: **Yes, ________________.**

2. A: **Are you a student?**

B: **Yes, ______________.**

3. A: **Are Manchester United and Tottenham Hotspur soccer teams?**

B: **Yes, ______________.**

4. A: **Is the NC Dinos your favorite team?**

B: **Yes, ______________.**

5. A: **Is Young-Mi your friend?**

B: **Yes, ______________.**

VIII. Complete the conversations.

1. A: **Is Chul-Soo a student?**

B: **No, __________________.**

2. A: **Are you a student?**

B: **No, __________________.**

3. A: **Are you students?**

B: **No, __________________.**

4. A: **Are Manchester United and Tottemhad Hotspur baseball teams?**

B: **No, ________________.**

5. A: **Is the NC Dinos your favorite team?**

B: **No, ________________.**

6. A: **Is Young-Hee your friend?**

B: **No, ________________.**

Remember this!

팀을 한 단체로 생각할 때는 팀을 대신할 수 있는 대명사는 it입니다. 반면에 팀 구성원을 생각할 때는 대명사 they를 사용합니다.

NC Dinos is my favorite team. I think it's the best baseball team. I like NC Dinos. They play well.

Vocabulary

일본	Japan		
중국	China	싱가포르	Singapore
베트남	Vietnam	말레이시아	Malaysia
태국	Thailand	독일	Germany
필리핀	the Philippines	호주	Australia
대만	Taiwan	인도네시아	Indonesia
미국	the United States (the U.S.)	캐나다	Canada

Pronunciation

Repeat after the teacher.

일본	Japan		
중국	China	싱가포르	Singapore
베트남	Vietnam	말레이시아	Malaysia
태국	Thailand	독일	Germany
필리핀	the Philippines	호주	Australia
대만	Taiwan	인도네시아	Indonesia
미국	the United States (the U.S.)	캐나다	Canada

Vocabulary

Country	Nationality
China	**Chinese (Chineses)**
Thailand	**Thai (Thais)**
Singapore	**Singaporean (Singaporeans)**
Germany	**German (Germans)**
Canada	**Canadian (Canadians)**
the Philippines	**Filipino (Filipinos)**
the United States (the U.S.)	**American (Americans)**
Japan	**Japanese (Japaneses)**
Taiwan	**Taiwanese (Taiwaneses)**
Malaysia	**Malaysian (Malaysians)**
Australia	**Australian (Australians)**
Indonesia	**Indonesian (Indonesians)**
Vietnam	**Vietnamese (Vietnameses)**

Pronunciation

Repeat after the teacher.

Thai (Thais)

Malaysian (Malaysians)

German (Germans)

American (Americans)

Australian (Australians)

Canadian (Canadians)

Chinese (Chineses)

Japanese (Japaneses)

Taiwanese (Taiwaneses)

Vietnamese (Vietnameses)

Filipino (Filipinos)

Indonesian (Indonesians)

Singaporean (Singaporeans)

Everyday Expressions!

Asking where someone is from
Where are you from?

Saying where you are from
I'm from Korea.
I'm Korean.
I'm a Korean.

I'm from Changwon, Korea.

Asking where someone is from	Saying where you are from
Where are you from?	I'm from Korea.
	I'm Korean.
	I'm a Korean.
	I'm from Changwon, Korea.

Remember this!

Where are you from?

이 질문은 국적, 거주지역, 출신 지역/나라를 물어볼 때 사용할 수 있습니다.

그러므로 이 질문에 아래와 같은 답변을 할 수 있습니다.
I'm from Korea.
(저는 한국에서 왔습니다.)
I'm Korean.
(저는 한국 국적의 사람입니다.)
I'm a Korean.
(저는 한국 사람입니다.)
I'm from Changwon. Korea.
(저는 한국 창원에서 거주하는 사람입니다.)

Pronunciation

Repeat after the teacher.

<table>
<tr><th>Asking where somone is from</th><th>Saying where you are from</th></tr>
<tr><td rowspan="4">Where are you from?</td><td>I'm from Korea.</td></tr>
<tr><td>I'm Korean.</td></tr>
<tr><td>I'm a Korean.</td></tr>
<tr><td>I'm from Changwon, Korea.</td></tr>
</table>

4 주차 2차시 학습:

Countries and Nationalities

Learning Objectives:

Name countries and nationalities.

Ask where someone is from.

Ask where someone or something is.

Grammar

QUESTIONS WITH WHO			SHORT ANSWERS
Who	's (is)	with you?	My mother (is)
		with Young-Chan?	I am.
			His mother (is)
			We are.
			His father and mother (are)

QUESTIONS WITH WHERE			SHORT ANSWERS
Where	are	you?	(I'm) at the beach. (We're) at the museum.
		they? your parents?	(They're) at the mall.
	is	he? she?	(He's/She's) in Taipei. (HE's/She's) at the hotel.
	's	Young-Chang? his mother?	
	is	it?	(It's) in Taipei, Taiwan.
	's	Taipei 101?	

Remember this!

I'm at the beach. 저는 해변가에 와있습니다.
We're at the museum. 우리는 박물관에 와있습니다.

It's In Taipei, Taiwan. 그것은 대만 타이페이에 있습니다.

at은 지역명이나 도시명 그리고 나라 이름을 제외한 특정 장소에 있다는 것을 말하고자 할 때 장소명 앞에서 사용됩니다. 반면에 **in**은 지역명, 도시명 그리고 국가명 앞에서 사용됩니다.

Pronunciation

Repeat after the teacher!

Who's with you?

My mother (is).

Who's with Young-Chan?

I am.

His mother (is).

We are.

His father and mother (are).

Where are you?

(I'm) at the beach.

(We're) at the museum.

Where are your parents? Where are they?

(They're) at the mall.

Where's Young-Chan? Where is he?

(He's) in Taipei.

Where's his mother? Where is she?

(She's) at the hotel.

Where's Taipei 101? Where is it?

(It's) in Taipei, Taiwan.

Let's check how much you understand!

Complete the conversation using *at*, *in* or *with*.

Young-Chan: **Hello?**

Min-Kyu: **Hi, Young-Chan. Where are you?**

Young-Chan: **Hi, Min-Kyu. I'm** __*in*__ **Taiwan.**

Min-Kyu: **Where ______ Taiwan?**

Young-Chan: **Taipei.**

Min-Kyu: **Really? Where exactly?**

Young-Chan: **We're ______ Taipei 101.**

Min-Kyu: **Who's ______ you?**

Young-Chan: **My mother.**

Min-Kyu: **That's great! Say "hello" for me.**

Speaking

Read the conversation with the teacher.

Young-Chan: **Hello?**

Min-Kyu: **Hi, Young-Chan. Where are you?**

Young-Chan: **Hi, Min-Kyu. I'm in Taiwan.**

Min-Kyu: **Where in Taiwan?**

Young-Chan: **Taipei.**

Min-Kyu: **Really? Where exactly?**

Young-Chan: **We're at Taipei 101.**

Min-Kyu: **Who's with you?**

Young-Chan: **My mother.**

Min-Kyu: **That's great! Say "hello" for me.**

Complete the questions with the information given in the parentheses. Then practice the conversation with the teacher.

You: ______________________________
(어디입니까?)

Teacher: **We're in Taiwan**.

You: ______________________________
(대만 어디입니까?)

Teacher: **Taipei.**

You: ______________________________
(정확하게 어디입니까?)

Teacher: **At Taipei 101**

You: ______________________________
(누구와 계십니까?)

Teacher: **My mother.**

Now answer the questions with the information given in the parentheses. Then practice the conversation with the teacher.

Teacher: **Are you from Korea?**

You: ______________________________

(네. 그래요.)

Teacher: **Where in Korea? Which city?**

You: ______________________________

(창원.)

Teacher: **Where exactly?**

You: ______________________________

(팔용동에서 삽니다. 어디에서 오셨습니까?)

Teacher: **I'm from Palyong-dong, too.**

You: ______________________________

(만나서 반갑습니다.)

What can you do now?

	Yes, I can	Mostly yes.	Not yet.
I can name countries and nationalities.			
I can ask where someone is from.			
I can ask where someone or something is.			

5 주차 1차시 학습:

Favorite Places in a City

Learning Objectives:

Talk about a city.

Talk about favorite places in the city.

Review

I. Fill in the blanks with *from*, *at*, or *in*.

1. The NC Dinos are ____ Changwon.

2. The baseball stadium is ____ Yangduk-dong.

3. I'm ____ the stadium.

4. We're ____ Gimhae now.

5. I'm ____ my favorite cafe ____ Yongho-dong.

II. Choose all the sentences that can be used to answer the question.

A: **Where are you from?**

B: ______________________

a. I'm Korean.
b. I'm a Korean.
c. I'm from Changwon.
d. I'm from Korea.

III. Complete the table.

Country	Nationality
Japan	Japanese
China	
	Vietnamese
	Taiwanese
	Malaysian
	Singaporean
the Philippines	
Indonesia	
the United State (the U.S.)	
Australian	
Canada	
Germany	

IV. Repeat after the teacher.

Where are you?

(I'm) at the beach.

(We're) at the museum.

Where are your parents? Where are they?

(They're) at the mall.

Where's Young-Chan? Where is he?

(He's) in Taipei.

Where's his mother? Where is she?

(She's) at the hotel.

Where's Taipei 101? Where is it?

(It's) in Taipei, Taiwan.

Vocabulary

tall	높이가 _____인
large	큰
big	큰
small	작은, 좁은
new	새로운
old	오래된
beautiful	아름다운
wonderful	아주 멋진
popular	평판이 좋은
famous	유명한
friendly	친절한, 상냥한
busy	바쁜, 번화한
crowded	붐비는
relaxing	편안한
exciting	신나는
interesting	흥미로운
fun	재미있는
boring	지루한

Let's check how you understand!

Complete the sentences using the vocabulary in the box.

wonderful	famous	boring	relaxing	fun
busy	old	crowded	tall	exciting
interesting	beautiful	friendly		

1. Yong-gee Lake Park is in Yongho-dong, Changwon. It's a ____________ place.

2. Muhak Mountain is 761 (seven hundred and sixty one) meters __________. There's a _______________ view of the city.

3. Masan Ursijang is an __________ fish market. It's __________ for seafood restaurants.

4. Jinhae Cherry Blossom Festival is in Spring. The streets in Jinhae are ____________ and ______________ with people from all over South Korea during the festival.

5. Moonshin Art Museum is _______________________. There are sculptures of Moonshin.

6. Gyeongju World is an ___________ place. There are some __________ rides.

Remember this!

관사 a 다음에 올 수 있는 단어는 자음 소리로 시작하는 단어이어야 합니다. 그리고 관사 an 다음에 올 수 있는 단어는 모음 소리로 시작하는 단어이어야 합니다.

Everyday Expressions!

Asking about favorite places

What is your favorite place in your city?

Why?

Where is it?

How is it?

Describing favorite places

It's Yong-gee Lake Park.

It's in Yongho-dong, Changwon.

It's relaxing.

Asking about favorite places	Describing favorite places
What's your favorite place in your city?	**It's Yong-gee Lake Park.**
Where is it?	**It's in Yongho-dong, Changwon.**
How is it?	**It's relaxing.**
Why?	

Pronunciation

Repeat after the teacher.

<table>
<tr><th>Asking about favorite places</th><th>Describing favorite places</th></tr>
<tr><td>What's your favorite place in your city?</td><td>It's Yong-gee Lake Park</td></tr>
<tr><td>Where is it?</td><td>It's in Yongho-dong, Changwon.</td></tr>
<tr><td>How is it?</td><td rowspan="2">It's relaxing.</td></tr>
<tr><td>Why?</td></tr>
</table>

5 주차 2차시 학습:

Favorite Places in a City

Learning Objectives:

Talk about a city

Talk about favorite places in the city.

Grammar

ADJECTIVES WITH *BE*			
	BE	ADJECTIVE	
Gyeongju World	is	exciting.	
The streets in Jinhae	are	busy	during the festival.
Moonshin Art Museum	is	interesting.	

Find the sentences that look like these, and underline them.

1. Yong-gee Lake Park is in Yongho-dong, Changwon. It's a relaxing place.

2. Muhak Mountain is 761 (seven hundred and sixty one) meters tall. There's a wonderful view of the city.

3. Masan Ursijang is an old fish market. It's famous for seafood restaurants.

4. Jinhae Cherry Blossom Festival is in Spring. The streets in Jinhae are crowded and busy with people from all over South Korea during the festival.

5. Moonshin Art Museum is interesting. There are famous sculptures of Moonshin.

6. Gyeongju World is an exciting place. There are some fun rides.

ADJECTIVES WITH *BE*				
	BE		ADJECTIVE	
It	**'s (is)**	**a**	**popular**	**place.**
There	**'s (is)**	**an**	**old**	**fish market.**
There	**are**		**famous**	**sculptures of Moonshin.**

Find the sentences that look like these, and underline them.

1. Yong-gee Lake Park is in Yongho-dong, Changwon. It's a relaxing place.

2. Muhak Mountain is 761 (seven hundred and sixty one) meters tall. There's a wonderful view of the city.

3. Masan Ursijang is an old fish market. It's famous for seafood restaurants.

4. Jinhae Cherry Blossom Festival is in Spring. The streets in Jinhae are crowded and busy with people from all over South Korea during the festival.

5. Moonshin Art Museum is interesting. There are famous sculptures of Moonshin.

6. Gyeongju World is an exciting place. There are some fun rides.

Pronunciation

Repeat after the teacher.

1. Yong-gee Lake Pakr is in Yongho-dong, Changwon.

It's a relaxing place.

2. Muhak Mountain is 761 (seven hundred and sixty one) meters tall.

There's a wonderful view of the city.

3. Masan Ursijang is an old fish market.

It's famous for seafood restaurants.

4. Jinhae Cherry Blossom Festival is in Spring.

The streets in Jinhae are crowded

and busy with people from all over South Korea during the festival.

5. Moonshin Art Museum is interesting.

There are famous sculptures of Moonshin.

6. Gyeongju World is an exciting place. There are some fun rides.

Speaking

Let's talk about Yong-gee Lake Park! First complete the conversation with the information below. Then practice the conversation with the teacher.

Yong-gee Lake Park is in Yongho-dong, Changwon. It's a relaxing place.

Teacher: **What's your favorite place in Changwon?**

You: ______________________________

Teacher: **Where is it?**

You: ______________________________

Teaher: **How is it?**

You: ______________________________

Now let's talk about Moonshin Art Museum! First complete the conversation with the information below. Then practice the conversation with the teacher.

Moonshin Art Museum is interesting. It's in Chusan-dong, Changwon. There are famous sculptures of Moonshin.

Teacher: **What's your favorite place in Changwon?**

You: ______________________________

Teacher: **Why?**

You: ______________________

Teaher: **Where is it?**

You: ______________________

Finally let's talk about Masan Ursijang! First complete the conversation with the information below. Then practice the conversation with the teacher.

Masan Ursijang is an old fish market. It's in Dongsur-dong. It's famous for seafood restaurants. The food is good.

Teacher: **What's your favorite place in Changwon?**

You: ______________________

Teacher: **Why?**

You: ______________________

Teaher: **Where is it?**

You: ______________________

What can you do now?

	Yes, I can	Mostly yes.	Not yet.
I can talk about a city.			
I can talk about my favorite places in the city.			

6 주차 1차시 학습:

Gifts

Learning Objectives:

Share information about the gifts you have received.

Give and reply to thanks.

Review

I. Fill in the blanks with *a*, *an*, or *nothing*.

1. It's _______ small cafe.

2. The park is _______ large.

3. The people of Gyeongsangnam-do are _______ friendly.

4. It's _______ interesting art museum,

5. There are _______ fun rides.

II. Unscramble the sentences.

1. food/the/good/is/.

____

2. the/is/exciting/music/.

____

3. famous/Jinhae/for/cherry blossoms/is/.

____

4. crowded/streets/the/are/.

____

5. cherry blossoms/beautiful/are/.

____

III. Choose all the sentences that can be used to answer the question.

A: What's your favorite place in Changwon?

B: ______________________________

a. It's in Yongho-dong.

b. It's Moonshin Art Museum.

c. It's Garosu-gil in Changwon.

d. It's from Changwon.

IV. Choose all the sentences that can be used to answer the question.

A: **Where is it?**

B: ______________________________

a. It's in Yongho-dong.

b. It's Moonshin Art Museum.

c. It's Garosu-gil in Changwon.

d. It's from Changwon.

V. Choose all the sentences that can be used to answer the question.

A: **How is it?**

B: ______________________________

a. It's in Yongho-dong.

b. It's interesting.

c. It's relaxing.

d. It's exciting.

Vocabulary

a smartwatch (smartwatches)	스마트워치
a backpack (backpacks)	배낭
a laptop (laptops)	노트북
a giftcard (gift cards)	기프트 카드
a wallet (wallets)	새로운
sunglasses	썬글라스
headphones	해드폰
cool	멋진
beautiful	아름다운, 맘에 드는
great	멋진
nice	보기 좋은, 맘에 드는
perfect	완벽한, 더 좋을 수 없는

Grammar

SPELLING RULES FOR FORMING PLURAL NOUNS	
~consonant + y	dictionary → dictionaries
~consonant + o	tomato → tomatoes potato → potatoes (photo → photos)
~ch **~sh** **~ss** **~x**	church → churches tooth brush → tooth brushes class → classes tax → taxes
~f **~fe**	leaf → leaves knife → knives

Let's check how much you understand!

Write the plural forms of the following nouns.

SINGULAR FORMS	PLURAL FORMS
a class	
a watch	
a dish	
a bus	
a backpack	
a notebook	
a laptop	
a wallet	
a camera	
a key	
an ID card	
an umbrella	

Remember this!

복수형의 명사들을 발음할 때 유의할 점:

1. 단수형 명사의 끝소리가 /s/, /z/, /ʃ/, /ʒ/, /tʃ/, /dʒ/, /ks/의 소리 중 하나라면 그 명사의 복수형 끝소리는 /ɪz/입니다.

단수형	단어의 끝소리	복수형	단어의 끝소리
a class	/s/	classes	/ɪz/
a quiz	/z/	quizzes	/ɪz/
a dish	/ʃ/	dishes	/ɪz/
a garage	/ʒ/	garages	/ɪz/
a watch	/tʃ/	churches	/ɪz/
a sausage	/dʒ/	sausages	/ɪz/
a fax	/ks/	faxes	/ɪz/

2. 단수형 명사의 끝소리가 무성음(/p/, /t/, /k/, /f/, or /θ/)이라면 그 명사의 복수형인 경우는 끝소리가 /s/입니다.

단수형	단어의 끝소리	복수형	단어의 끝소리
a laptop	/p/	laptops	/s/
a wallet	/t/	wallets	/s/
a notebook	/k/	notebooks	/s/
a roof	/f/	roofs	/s/
a path	/θ/	paths	/s/

3. 단수형 명사의 끝소리가 유성음(/b/, /d/, /g/, /l/, /m/, /n/, /ŋ/, /r/, /D/, /ð/, /v/, 그리고 모음)이라면 그 명사의 복수형인 경우는 끝소리가 /z/입니다.

예:
cameras, keys, ID cards, 그리고 umbrellas의 끝소리는 /z/입니다.

Pronunciation

Repeat after the teacher.

SINGULAR FORMS	PLURAL FORMS
a class	classes
a watch	watches
a dish	dishes
a bus	buses
a backpack	backpacks
a notebook	notebooks
a laptop	laptops
a wallet	wallets
a camera	cameras
a key	keys
an ID card	ID cards
an umbrella	umbrellas

Let's check how much you understand!

Complete the conversation.

A: **What are your gifts?**

B: **My gifts are** *a laptop* **(laptop), two** ____________**(sunglass)**

and __________________ **(headphones)**

A: **What's your favorite?**

B: **It's** ____________________ **(laptop)**

Remember this!

한 번 언급된 명사구를 다시 가리킬 때는 그 명사구 앞에 관사 the를 사용해야 합니다. 또는 대명사 'it'이나 'them'을 사용하여 앞에 언급된 명사구를 가리킬 수 있습니다.

예:

1. a. I have **an apple**. I can't share **the apple** with you because that's my lunch.
   b. I have **an apple**. I can't share **it** with you because that's lunch.

2. a. I have **some cookies** in the fridge. I'm going to have **the cookies** with coffee.
   b. I have **some cookies** in the fridge. I'm going to have **them** with coffee.

6 주차 2차시 학습:

Gifts

Learning Objectives:

Share information about the gifts you have received.

Give and reply to thanks.

Everyday Expressions!

Saying thank you

Thank you very much. FORMAL

Thank you.

Thanks a lot.

Thanks. INFORMAL

Replying to 'Thank you.'

You're welcome. FORMAL

My pleasure.

Sure. No problem.

You bet. (No problem.) INFORMAL

Saying thank you	Replying to 'Thank you.'
Thank you very much.	**You're welcome.**
Thank you	**My pleasure.**
Thanks a lot.	**Sure. No problem.**
Thanks.	**You bet.**

Pronunciation

Repeat after the teacher.

Saying thank you	Replying to 'Thank you.'
Thank you very much.	You're welcome.
Thank you	My pleasure.
Thanks a lot.	Sure. No problem.
Thanks.	You bet.

Remember this!

1. 대체로 친분이 있는 사람과 대화할 때나 사적인 자리에서는 완전한 문장으로 인사를 하지 않아도 됩니다. 위의 표현 중에서 'My pleasure!'와 'No problem. '은 완전한 문장이 아닙니다. 완전한 문장이 되려면 아래와 같이 표현해야 합니다.

'My pleasure.' → 'It was my pleasure.'
'No problem.' → 'It was no problem at all.'

2. 위의 문장에서 'You bet.'와 비슷한 의미가 있는 표현은 'My pleasure. '입니다. 그러므로 기쁜 마음으로 했으며 다음에도 기쁜 마음으로 해줄 수 있으니 너무 부담스러워하지 말라는 의미를 표현한 것입니다.

Everyday Expressions!

Saying thank you for a gift

Thanks. I really like it/them.

Thanks. I like it/them a lot.

It's cool/beautiful/great/nice/perfect.

They're cool/beautiful/great/nice/perfect

Replying to 'Thank you.'

I'm glad you like it.

I'm glad you like them.

Remember this!

1. 한 개의 선물이거나 선물이 짝을 이루는 물건이 아닐 때 사용할 수 있는 표현:

Thanks. I really like it.

It's cool/beautiful/great/nice/perfect.

I'm glad you like it.

2. 여러 개의 선물이거나 선물이 짝을 이루는 물건일 때 사용할 수 있는 표현:

Thanks. I really like them.

They're cool/beautiful/great/nice/perfect.

I'm glad you like them.

Pronunciation

Repeat after the teacher.

Thanks. I really like it.

Thanks. I really like them.

Thanks. I like it a lot.

Thanks. I like them a lot.

It's cool/beautiful/great/nice/perfect.

They're cool/beautiful/great/nice/perfect

I'm glad you like it.

I'm glad you like them.

Let's check how much you understand!

Complete the conversation.

Min-Kyu: **What's this?**

Young-Chan: **Happy Birthday. It's for you.**

Min-Kyu: **What's in the box?**

Young-Chan: **Open it, please.**

Min-Kyu: **Wow, they're sunglasses. Thanks, Young-chan.**

____

Young-Chan: **I'm glad you like them, Min-kyu.**

Min-Kyu: ________ **perfect.**

Pronunciation

Repeat after the teacher.

Min-Kyu: **What's this?**

Young-Chan: **Happy Birthday. It's for you.**

Min-Kyu: **What's in the box?**

Young-Chan: **Open it, please.**

Min-Kyu: **Wow, they're sunglasses. Thanks, Young-chan.**

I like them a lot. I really like them.

Young-Chan: **I'm glad you like them, Min-kyu.**

Min-Kyu: **They're perfect.**

Speaking

First complete the conversation with the information below. Then practice the conversation with the teacher.

You give the teacher a gift. It's a laptop.

Teacher: **What's this?**

You: ____________________

(선생님을 위해서 준비했어요. 생신을 축하드립니다.)

Teacher: **Wow! It's a laptop. Thank you. I like it a lot.**

You: ____________________

(마음에 드신다니 기쁩니다.)

Teacher: **It's perfect.**

Now complete the conversation with the information below. Then practice the conversation with the teacher.

The teacher gives you sunglasses as a gift.

You: ____________________

(이건 뭔가요?)

Teacher: **It's for you. Happy Birthday.**

You: ____________________

(와우! 썬글라스이네요. 감사합니다. 정말 마음에 듭니다.)

Teacher: **I'm glad you like them.**

You: ____________________

(마음에 드는 이유가 무엇일지 적어보세요.)

Remember this!

영어권 나라에서는 선물을 받아서 기뻐하는 모습을 보면서도 선물을 준비한 보람을 느끼지만, 마음에 드는 이유를 설명해 주면 선물을 준비한 사람은 더 기뻐하는 것 같습니다. 아래 표현의 의미를 참고하여 사용해 보세요.

It's cool. They're cool.	**멋진 선물입니다. (INFORMAL)**
It's beautiful. They're beautiful.	**아름다운 선물입니다.**
It's great. They're great.	**멋진 선물입니다.**
It's nice. They're nice.	**좋은 선물입니다.**
It's perfect. They're perfect.	**이보다 더 좋은 선물은 없을 겁니다. 제가 딱 원하던 선물입니다. 딱 맞네요. 선물이 (저에게) 잘 어울려요. 선물이 (저에게) 잘 맞아요.**

What can you do now?

	Yes, I can	Mostly yes.	Not yet.
I can share information about the gifts I have received.			
I can give and reply to thanks.			

7 주차 1차시 학습:

Items in the Classroom

Learning Objectives:

Describe important items in the classroom.

Talk about things that are near and not near.

Review

I. Correct the sentences.

1. There are two dictionary on the desk.

____

2. They're my favorite hat.

____

3. Your class are in Room 2051 and Room 2053.

____

4. I like tomatos.

____

5. There are two church on this street.

____

II. Unscramble the sentences.

1. I/ them/ really/ like/ .

____

2. like/ it/ lot/ I/ a/ .

____

3. your/ what/ gift/ favorite/ is/ ?

____

4. glad/ them/ I/ like/ 'm/ you/ .

____

5. you/ glad/ it/ like/ 'm/ I/ .

____

III. Choose all the sentences that can be used to complete the conversation.

A: **This is for you. Happy Anniversary!**
B: **Thank you. What's this?**
A: **Open it!**
B: ________________________________
A: **I'm glad you like them.**

a. Wow! It's a wallet. I really like it.
b. Wow! They're headphones. I like them a lot.
c. Wow! They're sunglasses. I really like them.
d. Wow! It"s a laptop. I like it a lot.

IV. Choose all the sentences that can be used to complete the conversation.

A: **Thank you.**
B: ________________________________

a. You're welcome.
b. My pleasure.
c. Sure. No problem.
d. You bet.

V. Choose all the sentences that can be used to complete the conversation.

A: **Thanks.**

B: ______________________________

a. You're welcome.

b. My pleasure.

c. Sure. No problem.

d. You bet.

VI. Choose all the sentences that can be used to complete the conversation.

A: **Thank you very much.**

B: ______________________________

a. You're welcome.

b. My pleasure.

c. Sure. No problem.

d. You bet.

VII. Choose all the sentences that can be used to complete the conversation.

A: **Thanks a lot.**

B: ______________________________

a. You're welcome.

b. My pleasure.

c. Sure. No problem.

d. You bet.

Vocabulary

a desktop computer	데스크톱컴퓨터
a laser projector	빔프로젝터
a whiteboard	칠판
a smart whiteboard	전자 칠판
a lectern	교탁
a smart lectern	전자교탁
a desk (desks)	책상
a chair (chairs)	의자
a board marker (board markers)	보드마커
a digital pen (digital pens)	디지털펜
an eraser (erasers)	지우개

clean	청결한
messy	정리 정돈이 안 된
expensive	값비싼
cheap	값싼
important	중요한
unimportant	중요하지 않은
good	좋은
bad	나쁜

Let's check how much you understand!

I. What's in a classroom? Complete the sentence using the words in the parentheses. Use *a* or *an* whenever it is needed.

In almost all classrooms, there are:

*a laser projector*__________(laser projector),

________________________(desktop computer),

________________________(whiteboard),

________________________(lectern),

________________________(desk),

and ______________________(chair).

II. How is your classroom? Complete the sentences using the words in the box.

clean	important	good	expensive	unimportant

1. It's not messy. It's ______________________.

2. A desktop computer and a laser projector are __________________. They're not cheap.

3. It's __________________ to have desks and chairs.

4. It's __________________ to have a smart whiteboard.

5. It's __________________ for students to have a smart lectern, but it's __________________ for teachers (to have a smart lectern).

Everyday Expressions!

Checking if the items in the classroom are important to have

Is it important to have a smart lectern in the classroom?

Is it important to have a smart lectern and a smart whiteboard in the classroom?

Describing the items in the classroom

It's very important to have a smart lectern in the classroom.

It's very important to have one (in the classroom).

It's very important to have a smart lectern and a smart whiteboard in the classroom.

It's very important to have them (in the classroom).

It's good to have a smart lectern in the classroom.

It's good to have one (in the classroom).

It's good to have a smart lectern and a smart whiteboard in the classroom.

It's good to have them (in the classroom).

Checking if the items in the classroom are important to have	Answering questions with more information
Is it important to have a smart lectern in the classroom?	Yes, it is. It's very important to have one.
	Not really. But it's good to have one.
It is important to have a smart lectern and a smart whiteboard in the classroom?	Yes, it is. It's very important to have them.
	Not really. But it's good to have them.

Remember this!

위의 문장에서 사용하는 'one'은 '그런 것 하나'라는 의미로 사용된 것입니다. 그 반면에 'them'은 질문에서 언급된 물건들을 가리킵니다.

one: 목적어로 사용될 때는 앞에 소개된 개념 또는 유사한 사물
it: 앞에 언급된 그 물건

예:
A: Do you have a pen?
B: I have one. (네가 말하는 것 하나 있어)

A: I can't find my bag. I don't know where it is.
B: Is this one yours? (이것, 네 것 맞니?)
A: Yes, it is. Thanks.

Pronunciation

Repeat after the teacher.

Is it important to have a smart lectern in the classroom?

Yes, it is. It's very important to have one.

Not really. But it's good to have one.

It is important to have a smart lectern and a smart whiteboard

in the classroom?

Yes, it is. It's very important to have them.

Not really. But it's good to have them.

7 주차 2차시 학습:

Items in the Classroom

Learning Objectives:

Describe important items in the classroom.

Talk about things that are near and not near.

Grammar

THIS/THAT/THESE/THOSE		
	Near	Not Near
Singular	**This** is a gift card.	**That**'s an expensive watch.
Plural	**These** credit cards are really good.	A: Are **those** your keys? B: Yes, they are.

THIS/THAT/THESE/THOSE		
	Near	Not Near
Singular	A: Yoon-Kyu, **this** is my friend Young-chan. B: Hi, Young-Chan. Nice to meet you.	A: Who's **that** over there? B: **That**'s Min-Kyu.
Plural	A: **These** are my parents. B: Nice to meet you, Mr. and Mrs. Kim.	A: Are **those** your friends? B: Yes, they are.

Let's check how much you understand!

Complete the sentences with *this*, *that*, *these*, or *those*.

1. Look! ________ is a new eraser. It's really good.

2. A: **Who's ________ over there?**

B: **That's my brother.**

3. ______________ book over there are interesting.

4. A: **I like your shoes.**

B: ____________ **shoes are really comfortable.**

Everyday Expressions!

Asking about the items in the classroom.

What's this?

What's that?

What are these?

What are those?

Explaining the items in the classroom.

This is a smart lectern	(It's a smart lectern.)
That's a laser projector.	(It's a laser projector.)
These are board markers.	(They're board markers.)
Those are erasers.	(They're erasers.)

Asking about the items in the classroom	Answering questions about the classroom.
What's this?	**It's a smart lectern.**
What's that?	**It's a laser projector.**
What are these?	**They're board markers.**
What are those?	**They're erasers.**
	Explaining the items in the classroom
	This is a smart lectern.
	That's a laser projector.
	These are board markers.
	Those are erasers.

Remember this!

this, that, these, 그리고 those의 첫소리는 /ð/입니다. 혀끝을 윗니에 댄 상태로 준비하고, 유성음이므로 성대를 진동시키면서 발음합니다. think의 첫소리와 다릅니다. think의 첫소리는 /θ/입니다. /ð/와 입 모양은 같지만, 성대를 진동시키지 않고 발음합니다.

Pronunciation

Repeat after the teacher.

What's this?

It's a smart lectern.

What's that?

It's a laser projector.

What are these?

They're board markers.

What are those?

They're erasers.

This is a smart lectern.

That's a laser projector.

These are board markers.

Those are erasers.

Speaking

First complete the conversation with the information below. Then practice the conversation with the teacher.

You: ____

(이것은 뭔가요?)

Teacher: **It's a smart lectern.**

You: ____

(저것은 뭔가요?)

Teacher: **It's a laser projector.**

You: ____

(이것은 다 뭔가요?)

Teacher: **They're board markers.**

You: ____

(저것은 다 뭔가요?)

Teacher: **They're erasers.**

Again complete the conversation first. Then practice the conversation with the teacher.

You: ______________________________

(이것은 뭔가요?)

Teacher: **It's a smart whiteboard.**

You: ______________________________

(이것이 있는 것이 중요한가요?)

Teacher: **Not really. But it's good to have one.**

You: ______________________________

(저것은 뭔가요?)

Teacher: **It's a laser projector.**

You: ______________________________

(저것이 있는 것이 중요한가요?)

Teacher: **Yes, it is. It's very important.**

Let's practice more. Complete the conversation first. Then practice the conversation with the teacher.

You: ______________________________
(지현아, 내 동생 윤규야.)

Teacher: **Nice to meet you, Yoon-Kyu.**

Yoon-Kyu: **Nice to meet you, too.**______________________

You: ______________________________
(우리 부모님이야.)

Teacher: **Nice to meet you, Mr. and Mrs. Park.**

Mr. and Mrs. Park: **Nice to meet you, too.**

Let's practice one more time. Complete the conversation first. Then practice the conversation with the teacher.

Teacher: **I like that photo on the wall. Are those your friends?**

You: ______________________________

(아닙니다. 저의 형제들입니다.)

Teacher: **This is a nice photo. Who's this?**

You: ______________________________

(저의 어머님입니다.)

What can you do now?

	Yes, I can	Mostly yes.	Not yet.
I can describe important items in the classroom.			
I can talk about things that are near and not near.			

8 주차 1차시 학습:

Daily Activities

Learning Objectives:

Explain what you are doing.

Greet people and ask how they are.

Review

I. Correct the sentences.

1. What's those?

____

2. It's eraser.

____

3. This is my friends.

____

4. Those is my pen.

____

5. They're not my sunglass.

____

II. Choose all the sentences that can be used to answer the question.

A: **What's this?**
B: ______________________________

a. It's a smart whiteboard.
b. They're board markers.
c. They're erasers.
d. It's a smart lectern.

III. Choose all the sentences that can be used to answer the question.

A: **What's that?**

B: ______________________________

a. It's a smart whiteboard.
b. They're board markers.
c. They're erasers.
d. It's a laser projector.

IV. Choose all the sentences that can be used to answer the question.

A: **What are these?**

B: ______________________________

a. It's a smart whiteboard.
b. They're board markers.
c. They're erasers.
d. It's a smart lectern.

IV. Choose all the sentences that can be used to answer the question.

A: **What are those?**

B: ______________________________

a. It's a smart whiteboard.
b. They're board markers.
c. They're erasers.
d. It's a laser projector.

Vocabulary

study for a test	시험 공부하다
watch YouTube	YouTube를 보다
text a friend	친구에게 문자 보내다
exercise (work out)	운동하다
listen to music	음악을 듣다
talk on the phone	전화로 통화하다
eat/ eat lunch	먹다/ 점심을 먹다
drink/ drink coffee	마시다/ 커피를 마시다
go to school	학교에 가다
shop	쇼핑하다
play online games	온라인게임을 하다

Let's check how much you understand!

Complete the sentences using the words in the box.

studying	watching	going	texting	listening
eating	playing	shopping	talking	drinking

1. We're ________________ at the mall.

2. I'm ________________ a friend.

3. They're ________________ to music.

4. I'm ________________ on the phone.

5. She's ________________ to school.

6. We're ________________ for the mid-term exams.

7. They're ________________ online games.

8. He's ________________ YouTube.

9. I'm ________________ lunch.

10. She's ________________ iced Americano.

Pronunciation

Repeat after the teacher.

1. We're shopping at the mall.

2. I'm texting a friend.

3. They're listening to music.

4. I'm talking on the phone.

5. She's going to school.

6. We're studying for the mid-term exams.

7. They're playing online games.

8. He's watching YouTube.

9. I'm eating lunch.

10. She's drinking iced Americano.

Grammar

THE PRESENT CONTINUOUS: AFFIRMATIVE AND NEGATIVE STATEMENTS		
I'm/You're/She's/He's/We're/They're	(not)	listening to music.

THE PRESENT CONTINUOUS: YES/NO QUESTIONS				
BE		VERB + ~ing	SHORT ANSWERS	
Are	**you**	**studying?**	**Yes**, I am.	**No**, I'm not.
Are	**you**		**Yes**, we are.	**No**, we're not. (No, we aren't.)
Is	**she** (Young-Hee)		**Yes**, she is.	**No**, she's not. (No, she isn't.)
Is	**he** (Chul-Soo)		**Yes**, he is.	**No**, he's not. (No, he isn't.)
Are	**they** (Young-Hee and Chul-Soo)		**Yes**, they are.	**No**, they're not. (No, they aren't.)

THE PRESENT CONTINUOUS: WH-QUESTIONS				
QUESTION WORD	**BE**		**VERB + ~ing**	**SHORT ANSWERS**
What	**are**	**you**	**doing?**	(I'm) **watching YouTube.**
	are	**you**		(We're) **watching YouTube.**
	's (is)	**she** (Young-Hee)		(She's) **watching YouTube.**
	's (is)	**he** (Chul-Soo)		(He's) **watching YouTube.**
	are	**they** (Young-Hee and Chul-Soo)		(They're) **watching YouTube.**
Who	**are**	**you**	texting?	(I'm texting) **my friend.**
	are	**you**		(We're texting) **our friends.**
	's (is)	**she** (Young-Hee)		(She's texting) **her friend.**
	's (is)	**he** (Chul-Soo)		(He's texting) **his friend.**
	are	**they** (Young-Hee and Chul-Soo)		(They're texting) **their friends.**

Remember this!

YES/NO 질문에 답을 할 때, 간단하게 YES 또는 NO로 대답할 수 있지만 친분이 없거나 상대방에게 예의를 갖춰서 대답할 때, 현재진행형 시제의 YES/NO 질문일 경우에는 위에서도 확인했지만, 아래와 같이 답을 합니다.

Are you studying?	Yes, I am. No, I'm not.
Are you studying?	Yes, we are. No, we're not. (No, we aren't.)
Is she studying? Is Young-Hee studying?	Yes, she is. No, she's not. (No, she isn't.)
Is he studying? Is Chul-Soo studying?	Yes, he is. No, he's not. (No, he isn't.)
Are they studying? Are Young-Hee and Chul-Soo studying?	Yes, they are. No, they're not. (No, they aren't.)

WH-의문사를 사용하는 질문에서도 짧게 답을 할 수 있지만, 친분이 없거나 상대방에게 예의를 갖춰서 대답해야 할 경우는 아래와 같이 완전한 문장으로 답을 합니다.

What are you doing?	I'm watching YouTube.
What are you doing?	We're watching YouTube.
What's she doing? What's Young-Hee doing?	She's watching YouTube.
What's he doing? What's Chul-Soo doing?	He's watching YouTube.
What are they doing? What are Young-Hee and Chul-Soo doing?	They 're watching YouTube.
Who are you texting?	I'm texting my friend.
Who are you texting?	We're texting our friends.
Who's she texting? Who's Young-Hee texting?	She's texting her friend.
Who's he texting? Who's Chul-Soo texting?	He's texting his friend.
Who are they texting? Who are Young-Hee and Chul-Soo texting?	They're texting their friends.

Let's check how much you understand!

Complete the conversations using the words in the parentheses. There can be more than one word in each blank.

1. A: ___________ **you** ___________ **YouTube (watch)?**

B: **Yes,** ___________ **am.**

2. A: ___________ **are** ___________ **doing?**

B: **We're** ____
(study for the exams).

3. A: ___________ **Chul-Soo** ________________________________
(playing an online games.)

B: **No,** ___________ **.**

A: ___________ **'s** ___________ **doing?**

B: **Listening to music.**

8 주차 2차시 학습:

Daily Activities

Learning Objectives:

Explain what you are doing.

Greet people and ask how they are.

Pronunciation

Repeat after the teacher.

POSITIVE SENTENCES
I'm studying.
You're studying.
She's studying.
He's studying.
We're studying.
They're studying.

NEGATIVE SENTENCES
I'm not studying.
You're not studying. (You aren't studying.)
She's not studying. (She's not studying.)
He's not studying. (She's not studying.)
We're not studying. (We aren't studying.)
They're not studying. (They' aren't studying.)

YES/NO QUESTIONS	SHORT ANSWERS	
Are you studying?	Yes, I am.	No, I'm not.
Are you studying?	Yes, we are.	No, we're not. No, we aren't.
Is Young-Hee studying? Is she studying?	Yes, she is.	No, she's not. No, she isn't.
Is Chul-Soo studying? Is he studying?	Yes, he is.	No, he's not. No, he isn't.
Are Youg-Hee and Chul-Soo studying? Are they studying?	Yes, they are.	No, they're not. No, they aren't.

WH- QUESTIONS	SHORT ANSWERS
What are you doing?	Watching YouTube.
What's Young-Hee doing? What's she doing?	
What's Chul-Soo doing? What's he doing?	
What are Youg-Hee and Chul-Soo doing? What are they doing?	

WH- QUESTIONS	SHORT ANSWERS
Who are you texting?	My friend.
Who are you texting?	Our friends.
Who's Young-Hee texting? Who's she texting?	Her friend.
Who's Chul-Soo texting? Who's he texting?	His friend.
Who are Youg-Hee and Chul-Soo texting? Who are they texting?	Their friends.

Everyday Expressions!

Greeting people and asking how they are
Hi. How are you?
Hi. How are you doing?

Greeting people and saying how you are
Okay./ Fine./ All right./ Pretty good. / How about you?
(Okay./ Fine./ All right./ Pretty good. And you?)

So-so. How about you?

Remember this!

위에 소개된 표현은 안부를 물어볼 때 사용합니다. 친분이 있는 사람들과 인사할 때만 사용하는 것이 아니라 공공장소에서도 모르는 사람들과도 이렇게 인사하는 것을 종종 확인할 수 있습니다. 예를 들면 마트 직원이 계산대에서 고객과 함께 이렇게 인사하는 것을 볼 수 있습니다. 그때는 아래와 같이 인사할 수 있습니다.

A: Hi. How are you today?
B: Fine. Thank you. How are you?
A: Pretty good. Thanks.

Pronunciation

Repeat after the teacher.

Hi. How are you?

Hi. How are you doing?

Okay./ Fine./ All right./ Pretty good. / How about you?

(Okay./ Fine./ All right./ Pretty good. And you?)

So-so. How about you?

Let's check how much you understand!

Complete the conversation.

Young-Hee: **Hi, Chul-Soo.** ______________________

Chul-Soo: **Fine.** ______________________

Young-Hee: **So-so.**

Chul-Soo: **What's wrong?**

Young-Hee: **I have exams next week.**

Chul-Soo: **You'll be all right.**

Youg-Hee: **Thanks.**

Pronunciation

Repeat after the teacher. After that practice the conversation with the teacher.

Young-Hee: **Hi, Chul-Soo. How are you doing?**

Chul-Soo: **Fine. How about you?**

Young-Hee: **So-so.**

Chul-Soo: **What's wrong?**

Young-Hee: **I have exams next week.**

Chul-Soo: **You'll be all right.**

Youg-Hee: **Thanks.**

Remember this!

친분이 있고 가까운 사이라면 위의 대화문에서처럼 현재 느끼는 감정 그대로 표현하면서 그렇게 느끼는 이유를 물어 볼 수 있습니다. 그때 위로하거나 격려하는 것으로 대화를 이어 나갈 수 있습니다. 그러나 잘 모르는 사이일 경우에는 Okay./ Fine./ All right./ Pretty good. 등을 사용하여 위에서 소개한 마트 직원과 고객이 나눈 인사처럼 짧게 인사를 나눌 수 있습니다.

Speaking

First complete the conversation with the information below. Then practice the conversation with the teacher.

You have exams soon. You are studying for them now. And you meet the teacher at the cafe in the library.

Teacher: **Hi. How are you doing?**

You: ______________________________

(잘 지내고 있습니다. 선생님은 어떠세요?)

Teacher: **Pretty good. What are you doing?**

You: ______________________________

(공부하고 있습니다.)

Teacher: **Oh! You have exams soon. Right?**

You: ______________________________

(맞습니다.)

Teacher: **Good luck!**

You: ______________________________

(감사합니다.)

What can you do now?

	Yes, I can	Mostly yes.	Not yet.
I can explain what I am doing.			
I can greet people and ask how they are.			

9 주차 1차시 학습:

These Days

Learning Objectives:

Talk about classes and university courses.

Talk about what you are doing these days.

Review

I. **Complete the conversation with the present continuous. Use contractions when they are possible, and use the words in the box.**

watch	listen	eat	study	talk	text

1. A: **What _____ you doing?**
   B: **I'm __________ YouTube.**

2. A: **_____ Young-Hee and Chul-Soo studying?**
   B: **No, they're not. They're __________ lunch.**

3. A: **_____ Yoon-Kyu __________ to music?**
   B: **No, he isn't. He's __________ a friend.**

4. A: **What _____ Min-Kyu doing?**
   B: **He's __________ on the phone.**

5. A: **What _____ they doing?**
   B: **They're __________ for a TOEIC test.**

II. Choose all the sentences that can be used to answer the question.

A: **What are you doing?**

B: ______________________________

a. I'm busy.
b. We're study for a quiz.
c. We're shopping at Shinsegye Department Store.
d. He's texting a friend.

III. Choose all the sentences that can be used to answer the question.

A: **Is Chul-Soo eating now?**

B: ______________________________

a. He's busy, now. He's shopping.
b. Yes, he is. He's eating a hamburger.
c. Yes, they are. They're at the cafeteria.
d. No, he isn't. He's in class now.

IV. Choose all the sentences that can be used to answer the question.

A: **How are you doing?**

B: ______________________________

a. Fine. How about you?
b. Not bad. How are you doing?
c. So-so. What's wrong?
d. How about you?

Vocabulary

study for a test	시험 공부하다
prepare for a test	시험을 준비하다
major in music	음악을 전공하다
study music	음악을 공부하다/음악을 전공하다
go to college	대학에 가다/대학에 다니다
take EnglishCommunicationI	EnglishCommunicationI을 수강하다
plan to go to Australia	호주에 가는 것을 계획하다

real estate business administration	부동산경영
computer software engineering	컴퓨터소프트웨어공학
fire and disaster prevention engineering	소방방재공학
food and nutrition	식품영양
police administration	경찰행정
cosmetology	미용(미용예술)
aviation hospitality	항공서비스
aircraft maintenance and mechanical engineering	항공정비기계공학

Pronunciation

Repeat after the teacher.

I'm studying real estate business administration.

You're studying computer software engineering.

He's studying fire and disaster prevention engineering.

She's studying food and nutrition.

They're studying police administration.

We're studying cosmetology.

He's studying aviation hospitality.

I'm studying aircraft maintenance and mechanical engineering.

Let's check how much you understand!

Complete the sentences using the words in the box.

preparing for	studying	planning to
taking	going to	majoring in

1. We're ______________________ the final exams.

2. I'm ______________________ food and nutrition.

3. They're ______________________ a writing class.

4. She's ______________________ have a birthday party for her sister.

5. We're ______________________ real estate business administration.

Remember this!

'She's going to have a birthday party for her sister.' 와 'She's planning to have a birthday party for her sister.' 는 다른 의미의 문장입니다.

She's going to have a birthday party for her sister.: 이 문장에서는 생일파티에 대한 준비가 이미 끝났고 이 행사가 임박했다는 것을 알 수 있습니다.

She's planning to have a birthday party for her sister.: 요즘 무엇을 하면서 지내는지 알려 주는 문장입니다. 생일파티를 위해서 계획하고 준비 중인 것을 알 수 있습니다.

9 주차 2차시 학습:

These Days

Learning Objectives:

Talk about classes and university courses.

Talk about what you are doing these days.

Pronunciation

Repeat after the teacher.

1. We're preparing for the final exams.

2. I'm majoring in food an nutrition.

3. They're taking a writing class.

4. She's planning to have a birthday party for her sister.

5. We're majoring in real estate business administration.

Grammar

THE PRESENT CONTINUOUS (EXTENDED TIME): AFFIRMATIVE AND NEGATIVE STATEMENTS		
I'm/You're/She's/He's/We're/They're	(not)	listening to music.

THE PRESENT CONTINUOUS (EXTENDED TIME): YES/NO QUESTIONS				
BE		VERB + ~ing	SHORT ANSWERS	
Are	**you**	**taking an online class this semester?**	**Yes**, I am.	**No**, I'm not.
Are	**you**		**Yes**, we are.	**No**, we're not. (No, we aren't.)
Is	**she** (Young-Hee)		**Yes**, she is.	**No**, she's not. (No, she isn't.)
Is	**he** (Chul-Soo)		**Yes**, he is.	**No**, he's not. (No, he isn't.)
Are	**they** (Young-Hee and Chul-Soo)		**Yes**, they are.	**No**, they're not. (No, they aren't.)

THE PRESENT CONTINUOUS (EXTENDED TIME): WH-QUESTIONS				
QUESTION WORD	**BE**		**VERB + ~ing**	**SHORT ANSWERS**
What	**are**	**you**	**doing these days?**	(I'm) **taking an online class.**
	are	**you**		(We're) **taking an online class.**
	's (is)	**she** (Young-Hee)		(She's) **taking an online class.**
	's (is)	**he** (Chul-Soo)		(He's) **taking an online class.**
	are	**they** (Young-Hee and Chul-Soo)		(They're) **taking an online class.**

Let's check how much you understand!

Complete the conversation with the present continuous. Use the words in the parentheses.

Young-Hee: **Hello!**

Chul-Soo: **Hi, Young-Hee! How are you doing?**

Youg-Hee: **Fine. How about you?**

Chul-Soo: **Pretty good. What ______ you ___________ (do) these days?**

Young-Hee: **I ________________________ (work) part-time at a movie theater.**

Chul-Soo: **Really? How is it?**

Young-Hee: **It's okay.**

Chul-Soo: **______ you ___________ (go) to school, too?**

Young-Hee: **Yes, I am.**

Chul-Soo: **Is it hard?**

Young-Hee: **Yes, it is. I ________________________ (study) in the evening after work.**

Chul-Soo: **You must be tired all the time.**

Young-Hee: **I am.**

Chul-Soo: **Sorry to hear that. Try to get some rest on the weekend.**

Young-Hee: **OK. Chul-Soo, my mother ____________________ (talk) to me. I have to go now.**

Chul-Soo: **No problem. Talk to you soon! Bye!**

Remember this!

위의 대화문은 Young-Hee와 Chul-Soo의 전화 통화 내용입니다. Young-Hee가 요즘 하는 일들과 지금 전화 통화 중에 일어나고 있는 일들을 표현하는 문장들이 있습니다.

Young-Hee가 요즘 하는 일들에 관한 실문과 실제로 요슴에 하는 일을 설명하는 문장:

What are you doing these days?

I'm working part-time at a movie theater.

Are you going to school, too?

I'm studying in the evening after work.

지금 통화 중에 일어나고 있는 일을 설명하는 문장:

My mother is talking to me.

이처럼 요즘 하는 일과 지금 잠시 일어나고 있는 일 모두 현재진행형 시제의 문장으로 표현할 수 있습니다. 맥락을 잘 파악하고 문장 끝에 있는 부사구(now, these days 등)를 확인하여 요즘 일어나는 일인지 아니면 지금 잠시 진행되고 있는 일인지 구분해야 합니다.

Pronunciation

Repeat after the teacher. After that, you play the role of Chul-Soo and read his lines, and your teacher will be Young-Hee. Finally, change roles.

Young-Hee: **Hello!**

Chul-Soo: **Hi, Young-Hee! How are you doing?**

Youg-Hee: **Fine. How about you?**

Chul-Soo: **Pretty good. What are you doing these days?**

Young-Hee: **I'm working part-time at a movie theater.**

Chul-Soo: **Really? How is it?**

Young-Hee: **It's okay.**

Chul-Soo: **Are you going to school, too?**

Young-Hee: **Yes, I am.**

Chul-Soo: **Is it hard?**

Young-Hee: **Yes, it is. I'm studying in the evening after work.**

Chul-Soo: **You must be tired all the time.**

Young-Hee: **I am.**

Chul-Soo: **Sorry to hear that. Try to get some rest on the weekend.**

Young-Hee: **OK. Chul-Soo, my mother is talking to me. I have to go now.**

Chul-Soo: **No problem. Talk to you soon! Bye!**

Remember this!

You **must be** tired all the time.
항상 피곤할 것 같습니다.

모든 상황을 파악하고 예측한 내용에 관하여 100% 확신이 있으면 사용하는 표현입니다.

다른 예:
You haven't eaten all day. You **must be** very hungry.
(하루 종일 먹지 못했군요. 매우 배가 고프겠습니다.)
That's a CHANNEL bag. It **must be** very expensive.
(그것은 샤넬 가방이군요. 매우 비싸겠습니다.)

Speaking

First complete the conversation with the information below. Then practice the conversation with the teacher.

You are going to school and studying music. You like it a lot.

Teacher: **What are you doing these days?**

You: ______________________________
(학교에 다닙니다.)

Teacher: **What are you studying?**

You: ______________________________
(음악 공부합니다.)

Teacher: **Great! Is it interesting?**

You: ______________________________
그렇습니다. 정말 재미있습니다.

Teacher: **That's great.**

You: ______________________________
(당신은요? 요즘 뭐 하십니까?)

Again complete the conversation with the information below. Then practice the conversation with the teacher.

You are taking an online class this semester. You are taking English Communication I.

Teacher: **Are you taking an online class this semester?**

You: ______________________________

(그렇습니다.)

Teacher: **Which one?**

You: ______________________________

(English Communication I을 수강하고 있습니다.)

What can you do now?

	Yes, I can	Mostly yes.	Not yet.
I can talk about classes and university courses.			
I can talk about what I am doing these days.			

10 주차 1차시 학습:

Food and Drinks

Learning Objectives:

Order food and drinks from a menu.

Talk about food and drinks you like and dislike.

Review

I. Choose all the sentences that can be used to answer the question.

A: **What are you doing this semester?**

B: ____________________

a. We're taking English Communication I.
b. We're going home.
c. We're shopping at Shinsegye Department Store.
d. I'm preparing for a TOEIC test.

II. Choose all the sentences that can be used to answer the question.

A: **What are you doing now?**

B: ____________________

a. I'm shopping at Shinsegye Department Store.
b. We're eating lunch.
c. We're taking English Communication I.
d. I'm in class.

III. Correct the sentences. The sentences should be in the present continuous tense.

1. They're shop at Lotte Department Store.

____

2. She waiting for a bus?

____

3. He is studying test.

____

4. I texting to my brother.

____

5. What he doing?

____

Vocabulary

a small salad	작은 양의 샐러드
a large salad	많은 양의 샐러드
vegetable soup and bread	야채수프와 빵
pasta with tomato sauce	토마토소스로 제조한 파스타
fried chicken	치킨
a burger with fries (burgers with fries)	감자튀김이 함께 나오는 햄버거
a chicken sandwich (chicken sandwiches)	오븐에서 구운 닭으로 만든 샌드위치
a drink (drinks)	음료
coffee	커피
juice	주스
soda	탄산음료
tea	차
water	물

Pronunciation

Repeat after the teacher.

A burger with fries.

A chicken sandwich with a small salad.

A burger and a soda.

Vegetable soup and bread.

Everyday Expressions!

Taking orders

Excuse me. Are you ready to order?
That comes with fries or a small salad. (What would you like?)
Anything to drink?
Anything else?

Ordering food

I'd like a chicken sandwich, please.
Fries, please.
I'd like a soda, please.
The same for me, please.
No, thanks. I think that's it.

Let's check how much you understand!

Complete the conversation with the expressions in the box.

Anything to drink? Excuse me. Are you ready to order? Anything else?

Young-Hee and Chul-Soo are at a food truck. A cook is taking their orders.

Cook:	______________________
Young-Hee:	**I'd like a chicken sandwich, please.**
Cook:	**That comes with fries or a small salad.**
Young-Hee:	**Fries, please.**
Cook:	**OK then. And you?**
Chul-Soo:	**The same for me, please.**
Cook:	**Two chicken sandwiches then.** __________
Young-Hee:	**I'd like a soda, please.**
Chul-Soo:	**Just water for me, please.**
Cook	**So you'd like two chicken sandwiches with fries, one soda and one water.**
Young-Hee:	**That's right.**
Chul-Soo:	**Oh, wait. Can I change my order? I'd like the salad, not fries.**
Cook:	**Got it. One chicken sandwich with the salad and one chicken sandwich with fries.** __________
Chul-Soo:	**No, thanks. I think that's it.**

Remember this!

위의 대화문에서도 확인했듯이 영어권 나라에서는 음식을 주문받을 때 동행자가 있으면 음식 주문을 각각 따로 받습니다. 그래서 각각 원하는 것을 말해주면 주문을 받은 사람은 주문한 내용을 잘 기억하고 음식을 주문한 사람에게 줍니다.

대게 음식이나 음료는 셀 수 없는 명사이지만 음식점에서는 셀 수 있는 명사처럼 사용합니다. 음식점마다 정해둔 기준으로 주문을 받기 때문인 것 같습니다.

At Home	At Eateries
Two cups of coffee, please	Two coffees, please.
Two bowls of soup, please.	Two soups, please.
Three large bowls of salad, please.	Three large salads, please.
One glass of water, please.	One water, please.
Two tall mugs of coffee, please.	Two tall coffees, please.
A glass of soda, please.	One soda, please.
A glass of orange juice, please.	One orange juice, please.
Two glasses of iced water please.	Two iced waters, please.
Some fries, please.	One fries, please.
Two plates of fries, please. (*)	Two servings of fries, please.

(*) Fries는 이미 복수형이기 때문에 감자튀김 두 개를 주문하려면 'two servings of fries'로 사용하면 의미가 더 정확히 전달될 것입니다. (1인분에 해당하는 양을 'one serving'이라고 표현합니다.) 그러므로 감자튀김을 작은 포장으로 두 개를 주문하려면 'two small servings of fries'라고 하면 됩니다.

Pronunciation

Repeat after the teacher. After that, practice the conversation with the teacher.

Cook: **Excuse me. Are you ready to order?**

Young-Hee: **I'd like a chicken sandwich, please.**

Cook: **That comes with fries or a small salad.**

Young-Hee: **Fries, please.**

Cook: **OK then. And you?**

Chul-Soo: **The same for me, please.**

Cook: **Two chicken sandwiches then. Anything to drink?**

Young-Hee: **I'd like a soda, please.**

Chul-Soo: **Just water for me, please.**

Cook **So you'd like two chicken sandwiches with fries, one soda and one water.**

Young-Hee: **That's right.**

Chul-Soo: **Oh, wait. Can I change my order?**

I'd like the salad, not fries.

Cook: **Got it. One chicken sandwich with the salad**

and one chicken sandwich with fries. Anything else?

Chul-Soo: **No, thanks. I think that's it.**

10 주차 2차시 학습:

Food and Drinks

Learning Objectives:

Order food and drinks from a menu.

Talk about food and drinks you like and dislike.

Grammar

THE SIMPLE PRESENT AFFIRMATIVE STATEMENTS		
SUBJECT PRONOUN	VERB	
I You We They	eat	meat
She He It	eats	

THE SIMPLE PRESENT NEGATIVE STATEMENTS			
SUBJECT PRONOUN		VERB	
I You We They	do not (don't)	eat	meat
She He It	does not (doesn't)	eats	

SPELLING RULES FOR THIRD PERSON SINGULAR (she. he. it)
You usually need to add *s* to the base form of the verb: **eat → eats**
If the base form ends in • **s, sh, ch, x, or z,** add **es** : **teach → teaches** • **a consonant + y,** change the **y** to **i** and add **es** : **study → studies** • **a consonant + o,** add **es :** **go → goes**

Pronunciation

Repeat after the teacher.

I eat meat.	I don't eat meat.
You eat meat.	You don't eat meat.
We eat meat.	We don't eat meat.
They eat meat.	They don't eat meat.
She eats meat	She doesn't eat meat.
He eats meat	He doesn't eat meat.
It eats meat.	It doesn't eat eat.

Let's check how much you understand!

Complete the sentences. Use the words in the parentheses.

1. Young-Hee *doesn't eat* (not/eat) breakfast. She just ____________(drink) coffee.

2. She __________(eat) Korean food for lunch. It's her favorite.

3. She ___________(know) a good Korean restaurant, but she ______________(eat) at the cafeteria.

4. After class, she _________(go) to a cafe and __________(study) there. She __________(drink) her favorite drink. It's a yogurt drink.

5. She _________(go) home after 6 and _________(eat) dinner with her family.

Pronunciation

Repeat after the teacher.

Young-Hee doesn't eat breakfast.

She just drinks coffee.

She eats Korean food for lunch.

It's her favorite.

She knows a good Korean restaurant, but she eats at the cafeteria.

After class, she goes to a cafe and studies there.

She drinks her favorite drink.

It's a yogurt drink.

She goes home after 6 and eats dinner with her family.

Everyday Expressions!

Asking for likes and dislikes

Do you like Vietnamese food?

Do you like soda?

Expressing likes an dislikes

I love it

I like it.

It's OK, but it's not my favorite.

Not really.

(I don't know. I haven't tried it yet.)

Remember this!

Statements	Meaning
I love it.	아주 많이 좋아합니다.
I like it.	좋아합니다.
It's OK, but it's not my favorite.	괜찮아요. 그렇지만 제가 제일 좋아하는 음식은 아닙니다.
Not really.	그렇게 많이 좋아하지 않습니다.
I don't know. I haven't tried it yet.	잘 모르겠습니다. 아직 먹지 못했습니다. (먹어 본 적이 없습니다.)

Pronunciation

Repeat after the teacher.

Do you like Vietnamese food?

Do you like soda?

I love it

I like it.

It's OK, but it's not my favorite.

Not really.

I don't know. I haven't tried it yet.

Remember this!

음식에 관해서 'Do you like it? '과 같은 질문을 받으면 싫어한다는 표현으로 'I don't like it.'나 'Not at all.'은 사용하지 않는 것 같습니다. 특별히 공적인 자리에서 친분을 쌓아야 하는 사람과 식사할 때 이런 질문을 받으면 단도직입적으로 싫어한다는 표현을 하기보다는 질문한 사람이 당황하지 않도록 아래의 표현을 대신 사용하는 것이 더 나을 것 같습니다.

It's OK, but it's not my favorite.
Not really.
I don't know. I haven't tried it yet.

Speaking

First complete the conversation with the information below. Then practice the conversation with the teacher.

You love Vietnamese food. And you haven't eaten Thai food yet.

Teacher: **Do you like Vietnamese food?**

You: ______________________________

(아주 많이 좋아합니다.)

Teacher: **How about Thai food?**

You: ______________________________

(잘 모르겠습니다. 먹어 본 적이 없습니다.)

Now complete the conversation with the information below. Then practice the conversation with the teacher.

You don't really like fast food, but you like fried chicken.

Teacher: **Do you like fast food?**

You: ____

(그렇게 많이 좋아하지 않습니다.)

Teacher: **How about fried chicken?**

You: ____

(그건 좋아합니다.)

What can you do now?

	Yes, I can	Mostly yes.	Not yet.
I can order food and drinks from a menu.			
I can talk about food and drinks I like and dislike.			

11 주차 1차시 학습:

Healthy Eating Habits

Learning Objectives:

Talk about healthy eating habits.

Talk about your favorite food.

Review

I. Complete the sentences with the simple present tense. Use the words in the parentheses, and use truncations when they are possible.

1. You ___*drink*___ (drink) coffee in the afternoon.

2. Young Hee ________________ (not/eat) seafood.

3. Chul-Soo ________ (eat) everything.

4. Young-Hee and Chul-Soo ________ (do) homework together.

5. They ________________ (not/drink) tea or coffee.

6. Chul-Soo ________ (study) in the library after school.

7. He ________ (go) home after six.

II. Choose all the sentences that can be used to answer the question.

A: **Are you ready to order?**

B: ____

a. I'd like a burger and fries, please.
b. Just water, please.
c. I don't know. I haven't tried it yet.
d. No, thanks. That's it.

III. Choose all the sentences that can be used to answer the question.

A: **Anything to drink?**

B: ____________________

a. I'd like a burger and fries, please.
b. Just water, please.
c. I don't know. I haven't tried it yet.
d. No, thanks. That's it.

IV. Choose all the sentences that can be used to answer the question.

A: **Anything else?**

B: ____________________

a. I'd like a burger and fries, please.
b. Just water, please.
c. I don't know. I haven't tried it yet.
d. No, thanks. That's it.

Vocabulary

skip meals	식사를 거르다
drink a lot of water	많으 양의 물을 마시다
eat snacks between meals	식사 사이에 간식을 먹다
eat a lot of cake and candy	많은 양의 케이크와 사탕을 먹다
eat breakfast/lunch/dinner	아침/점심/저녁을 먹다
eat a good breakfast	건강에 좋은 음식으로 만든 아침을 먹다
eat a lot of food before bedtime	자기 전에 많은 양의 음식을 먹다

It's good for you.	**그것은 당신에게 좋습니다.**
It's bad for you.	**그것은 당신에게 나쁩니다.**
It's healthy.	**그것은 건강에 좋습니다.**
It's unhealthy.	**그것은 건강에 좋지 않습니다.**
It's high in sugar.	**그것은 설탕 함유량이 많습니다.**
It's low in sugar.	**그것은 설탕 함유량이 적습니다.**
It tastes good.	**그것은 맛이 좋습니다. (그것은 맛있습니다.)**
It tastes bad	**그것은 맛이 나쁩니다. (그것은 맛없습니다.)**
It gives you energy.	**그것은 당신에게 에너지를 제공합니다.**

Let's check how much you understand!

I. Check the tips for healthy eating. If the tips are bad, rewrite the sentences and begin them with *Don't.*

______ **1.** Drink 6 or 8 glasses of water.

____

______ **2.** Drink a lot of soda.

____

______ **3.** Eat healthy snacks between meals.

____

______ **4.** Eat a lot of cake and candy.

____

______ **5.** Eat a good breakfast.

____

______ **6.** Eat a lot of food before bedtime.

____

______ **7.** Skip meals.

____

II. Give a good reason for each tip. Use the expressions in the box.

It's good for you.	It's bad for you.
It's high in sugar.	It's low in sugar.
It tastes good, but it's unhealthy.	It gives you energy.

1. Drink 6 or 8 glasses of water. ______________________

____

2. Don't drink a lot of soda. ______________________

____

3. Eat healthy snacks between meals. ______________________

____

4. Don't eat a lot of cake and candy. ______________________

____

5. Eat a good breakfast. ______________________

____

6. Don't eat a lot of food before bedtime. ______________________

____

7. Don't skip meals. ______________________

____

Pronunciation

Repeat after the teacher.

1. Drink 6 or 8 glasses of water. It's good for you.

2. Don't drink a lot of soda. It's high in sugar.

3. Eat healthy snacks between meals. It's good for you.

4. Don't eat a lot of cake and candy.

It tastes good, but it's unhealthy.

5. Eat a good breakfast. It gives you energy.

6. Don't eat a lot of food before bedtime. It's bad for you.

7. Don't skip meals. It's bad for you.

11 주차 2차시 학습:

Healthy Eating Habits

Learning Objectives:

Talk about healthy eating habits.

Talk about your favorite food.

Grammar

<table>
<tr><th colspan="4">YES/NO QUESTIONS</th><th>SHORT ANSWERS</th></tr>
<tr><td rowspan="6">Do</td><td rowspan="2">you</td><td rowspan="10">like</td><td rowspan="10">hot and spicy food?</td><td>Yes, I do.</td></tr>
<tr><td>No, I don't.
(No, I do not.)</td></tr>
<tr><td rowspan="2">you</td><td>Yes, we do.</td></tr>
<tr><td>No, we don't.
(No, we do not.)</td></tr>
<tr><td rowspan="2">they</td><td>Yes, they do.</td></tr>
<tr><td>No, they don't.
(No, they do not.)</td></tr>
<tr><td rowspan="4">Does</td><td rowspan="2">she</td><td>Yes, she does.</td></tr>
<tr><td>No, she doesn't.
(No, she does not.)</td></tr>
<tr><td rowspan="2">he</td><td>Yes, he does.</td></tr>
<tr><td>No, he doesn't.
(No, he does not.)</td></tr>
</table>

YES/NO QUESTIONS				SHORT ANSWERS
Does	it	taste	good?	Yes, it does.
				No, it doesn't. (No, it does not.)

Remember this!

No, I don't.
No, we don't.
No, they don't
No, she doesn't
No, he doesn't.
No, it doesn't.

위의 문장을 사용하여 전달하고자 하는 것보다 더 강하게 부정을 하고 싶을 때는 아래의 문장들을 사용하면 됩니다. 이 문장들에서 강세를 받는 단어들은 'No'와 'not'입니다.

No, I do **not**.
No, we do **not**.
No, they do **not**.
No, she does **not**.
No, he does **not**.
No, it does **not**.

Pronunciation

Repeat after the teacher.

Do you like hot and spicy food?
Yes, I do.
No, I don't.

Does she like hot and spicy food?
Yes, she does.
No, she does not.

Do you like hot and spicy food?
Yes, we do.
No, we don't.

Does he like hot and spicy food?
Yes, he does.
No, he doesn't.

Do they like hot and spicy food?
Yes, they do.
No, they don't.

Does it taste good?
Yes, it does.
No, it doesn't.

Let's check how much you understand!

Complete the conversation with Yes/No questions and answers using the words in the parentheses.

Min-Kyu: **What are you eating?**

Young-Chan: **Pasta with chocolate sauce.**

Min-Kyu: **Really? ______________________________ (it/taste) good?**

Young-Chan: **Yes, _____________ . I love it. ________________ ___________ (you/want) some?**

Min-Kyu: **No, thanks. I don't like chocolate.**

Young-Chan: **Min-Kyu, __________________________ (you/know) a good restaurant? My parents want to go to a nice one.**

Min-Kyu: **__________________________ (they/like) hot and spicy food?**

Young-Chan: **Well, my father _______ (like) it, but my mother doesn't.**

Min-Kyu: **__________________________ (they/eat) sushi?**

Young-Chan: **Yes, _____________ . They love it.**

Min-Kyu: **Try Sushiron. It's a good place.**

Pronunciation

Repeat after the teacher. After that, practice the conversation with the teacher.

Min-Kyu: **What are you eating?**

Young-Chan: **Pasta with chocolate sauce.**

Min-Kyu: **Really? Does it taste good?**

Young-Chan: **Yes, it does. I love it. Do you want some?**

Min-Kyu: **No, thanks. I don't like chocolate.**

Young-Chan: **Min-Kyu, Do you know a good restaurant?**

My parents want to go to a nice one.

Min-Kyu: **Do they like hot and spicy food?**

Young-Chan: **Well, my father like it, but my mother doesn't.**

Min-Kyu: **Do they eat sushi?**

Young-Chan: **Yes, they do. They love it.**

Min-Kyu: **Try Sushiron. It's a good place.**

Speaking

First complete the conversation with the information below. Then practice the conversation with the teacher.

You eat a good breakfast and have a lot of energy in the morning. You don't eat snacks between meals. You just have three good meals.

Teacher: **Do you eat breakfast?**

You: ____

(네, 먹습니다. 아침은 저에게 많은 에너지를 줍니다.)

Teacher: **Do you eat snacks?**

You: ____

(아니요. 먹지 않습니다. 그냥 세 끼만 챙겨 먹습니다.)

Teacher: **Do you ever skip meals?**

You: ____

(아니요 그러지 않습니다.)

Teacher: **Wow. You have a healthy eating habit.**

You: ____

(그러기를 바랄 뿐입니다.)

Again complete the conversation with the information below. Then practice the conversation with the teacher.

The teacher likes Chinese food, but it's high in carbs and calories. You like it, too. You like Jajangmyeon a lot. It's your favorite. (carbohydrates의 줄인 표현은 carbs이며 뜻은 탄수화물입니다.)

You: ______________________________
(중화요리 좋아하시나요?)

Teacher: **Yes, I do. I try not to eat it all the time.**

You: ______________________________
(왜요?)

Teacher: **It's high in carbs and calories.**

You: ______________________________
(그건 사실이에요.)

Teacher: **How about you? Do you like Chinese food?**

You: ______________________________
(저도 많이 좋아합니다. 제가 가장 좋아하는 것은 자장면입니다.)

Teacher: **That's my favorite, too.**

Remember this!

A: **Wow. You have a healthy eating habit.**
B: **I hope so.**

말하기를 연습하면서 접한 'I hope so.'는 '앞에 언급한 내용을 소망합니다'라고 직역할 수 있지만 문맥을 고려해서 번역한다면 '그러기를 바랄 뿐이다'의 의미가 있을 수 있습니다.

A: **Do you like Chinese food?**
B: **That's my favorite, too.**

바로 앞에서 말하기 연습한 내용 중에서 마지막 부분에 사용된 'That's my favorite, too'는 질문한 사람이 중식을 좋아한다고 했으니 저도 그렇다고 말하려면 'That's my favorite.'뒤에 'too'을 붙이면 됩니다.

What can you do now?

	Yes, I can	Mostly yes.	Not yet.
I can talk about healthy eating habits.			
I can talk about my favorite food.			

12 주차 1차시 학습:

Family

Learning Objectives:

Identify family members.

Talk about age.

Review

I. Complete the yes-no questions with the simple present tense. Use the words in the box.

give	eat	drink	taste	high

1. _______ you _______ 6 to 8 glasses of water?

2. _______ he _______ snacks between meals?

3. _______ it _______ in protein?

4. _______ it _______ you energy?

5. _______ they _______ a lot of food before bedtime?

6. _______ it _______ good?

7. _______ she _______ a lot of soda?

II. Choose all the sentences that can be used to respond to this statement.

A: **I eat cake after a good meal.**

B: ______________________________

a. Cake is high in sugar. It's unhealthy.
b. That's good for you.
c. That's bad for you.
d. That's healthy.

III. Choose all the sentences that can be used to respond to this statement.

A: **I eat a good breakfast everyday.**

B: ______________________________

a. I don't. But I think that's healthy.
b. That's great. A good breakfast is high in vitamins.
c. I do, too. It gives me a lot of energy in the morning.
d. Me, too. I think it is good for you.

Vocabulary

grandmother	할머니
grandfather	할아버지
grandparents	조부모
mother	어머니
father	아버지
parents	부모
husband	남편
wife	아내
daughter	딸
son	아들

a sister (sisters)	여동생, 언니, 누나
a brother (brothers)	남동생, 오빠, 형
an aunt (aunts)	이모, 고모, 숙모, 외숙모, 작은어머니, 큰어머니
an uncle (uncles)	이모부, 고모부, 삼촌, 외삼촌, 작은아버지, 큰아버지
a cousin (cousins)	사촌
a niece (nieces)	여 조카
a nephew (nephews)	남 조카
a grandchild (grandchildren)	손녀, 손자

Let's check how much you understand!

I. Complete the sentences about the family tree.

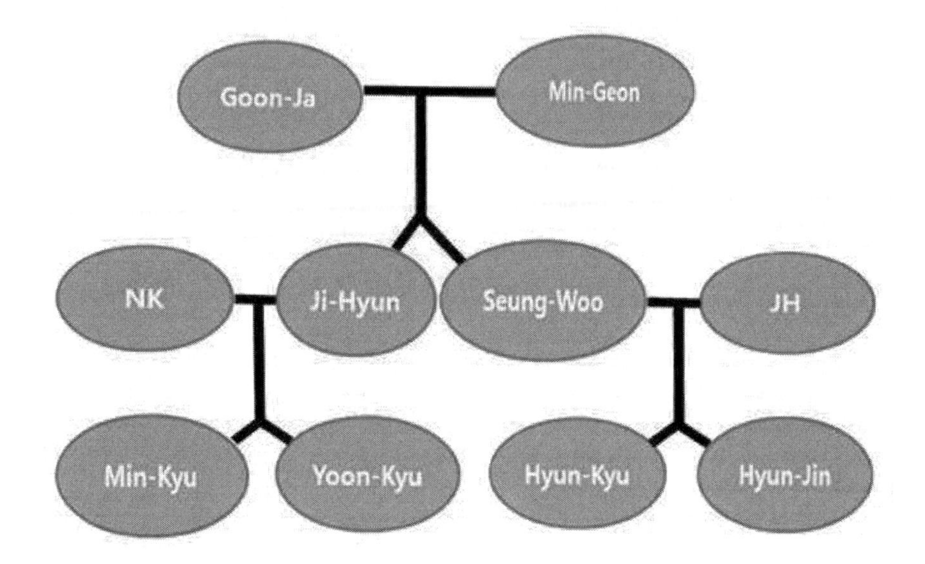

1. Hyun-Kyu and Hyun-Jin are brothers. Their aunt is ______________.

2. Their parents are ____________________ and ____________________.

3. Their cousins are ____________________ and ____________________.

4. Their uncle is ______________.

II. Complete the sentences about the family tree.

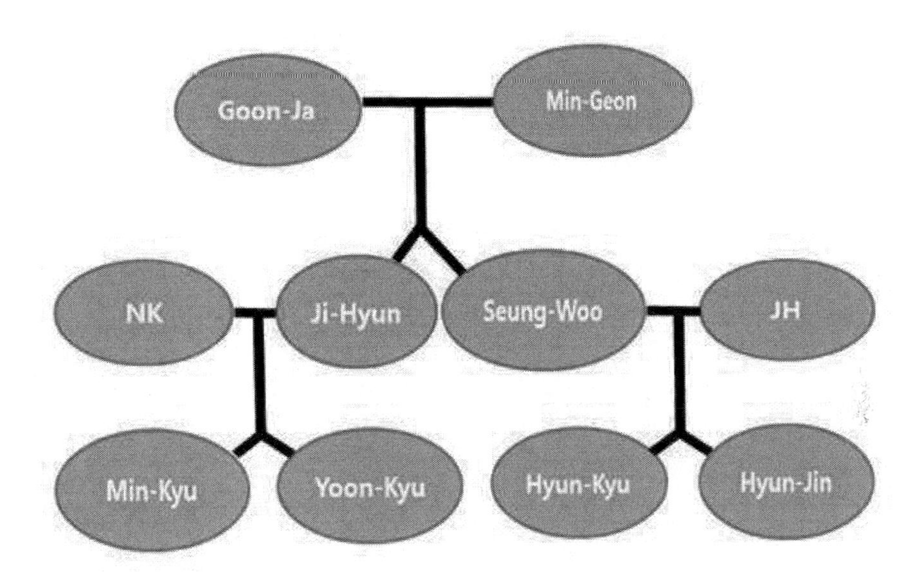

Goon-Ja and Min-Geon have ________ grandchildren. They are ______

____

____.

III. Complete the sentences about the family tree.

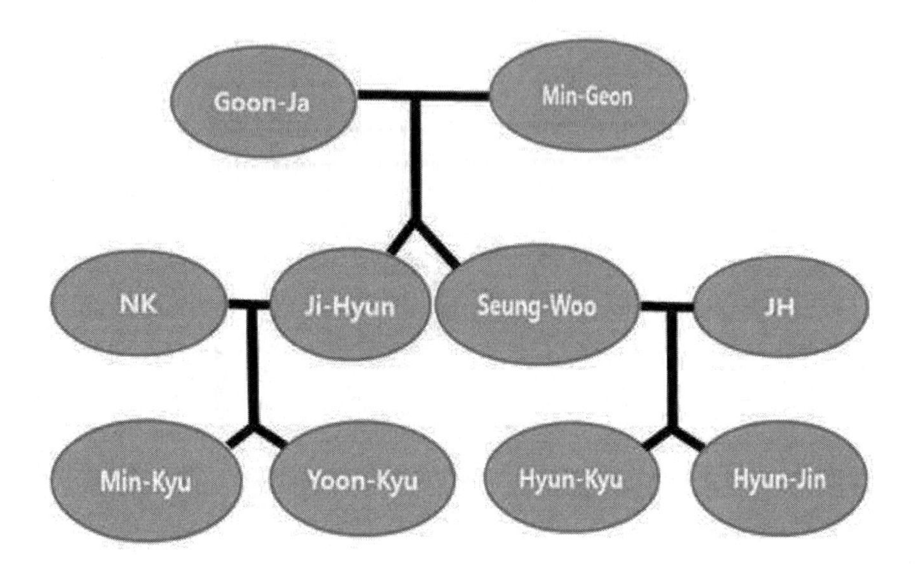

Goon-Ja and Min-Geun have a daughter and a son. ____________ is their daughter and ____________ is their son.

IV. Complete the sentences about the family tree.

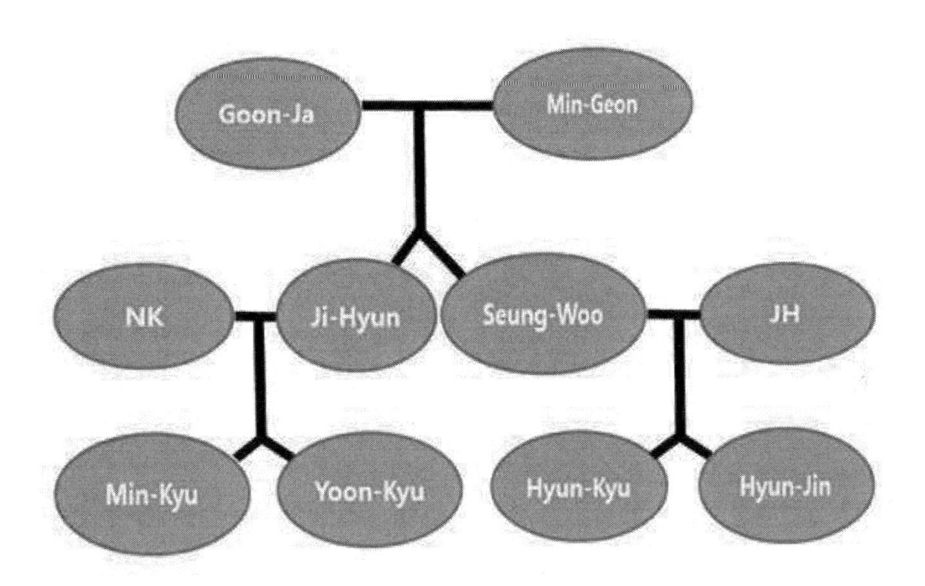

Ji-Hyun has __________ nephews. She doesn't have a ______________.

Pronunciation

Repeat after the teacher.

1. Hyun-Kyu and Hyun-Jin are brothers. Their aunt is Ji-Hyun.

2. Their parents are Seung-Woo and JH.

3. Their cousins are MIn-Kyu and Yoon-Kyu.

4. Their uncle is NK.

5. Goon-Ja and Min-Geon have four grandchildren.

They are Min-Kyu, Yoon-Kyu, Hyun-Kyu, and Hyun-Jin.

6. Goon-Ja and Min-Geon have a daughter and a son.

Ji-Hyun is their daughter and Seung-Woo is their son.

7. Ji-Hyun has two nephews. She doesn't have a niece.

12 주차 2차시 학습:

Family

Learning Objectives:

Identify family members.

Talk about age.

Grammar

POSSESSIVE NOUNS	
Singular nouns	Min-Kyu's brother is 22.
Plural nouns	Her nephews' names are Hyun-Kyu and Hyun-Jin.
Irregular plural nouns	Their grandchildren's names are Min-Kyu, Yoon-Kyu, Hyun-Kyu, and Hyun-Jin
Names ending in -s	Carlos's/Carlos' family's car is old.
More than two nouns	My mother and father's car is old. My brother's and sister's cars are new.

Remember this!

IRREGULAR PLURAL NOUNS	
SINGULAR	PLURAL
child	children
man	men
woman	women

Let's check how much you understand!

Complete the sentences using the family tree and the words in the parentheses.

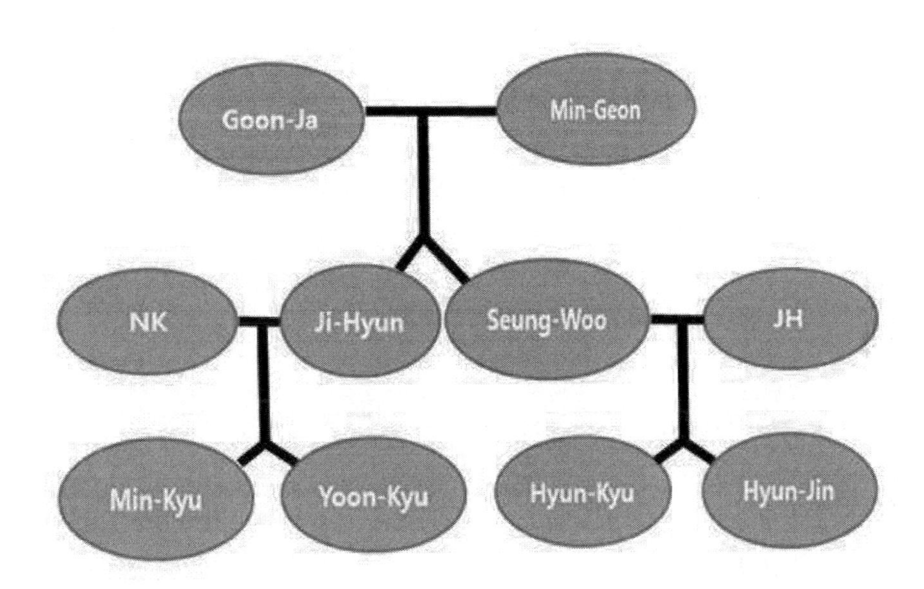

1. *Min-Kyu's* (Min-Kyu) cousins are Hyun-Kyu and Hyun-Jin.

2. Hyun-Kyu is ________________ and ________________ cousin.

3. ________________ (Goon-Ja) daughter is Ji-Hyun.

4. ________________ (Min-Kyu) and ________________ (Yoon-Kyu) cars are different.

5. NK and Ji-Hyun's ________________ (children) names are Min-Kyu and Yoon-Kyu.

Pronunciation

Repeat after the teacher.

1. Min-Kyu's cousins **are Hyun-Kyu and Hyun-Jin.**

2. **Hyun-Kyu is** Min-Kyu and Yoon-Kyu's cousin.

3. Goon-Ja's daughter **is Ji-Hyun.**

4. Min-Kyu's and Yoon-Kyu's cars **are different.**

5. NK and Ji-Hyun's children's names **are Min-Kyu and Yoon-Kyu.**

Remember this!

민규의 사촌들
→ Min-Kyu'**s** cousins

민규와 윤규의 사촌들
→ Min-Kyu and Yoon-Kyu'**s** cousins

민규의 자동차와 윤규의 자동차
→ Min-Kyu'**s** and Yoon-Kyu'**s** cars

NK와 지현이의 자녀들의 이름
→ NK and Ji-Hyun'**s** children'**s** names

Let's check how much you understand!

I. Complete the questions about Ji-Hyun using the words in the parentheses.

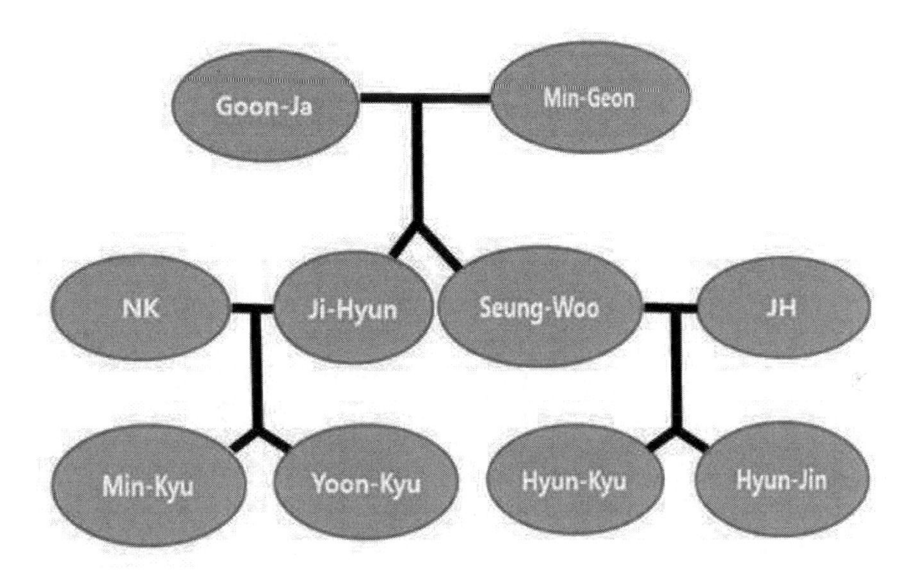

1. What are her (parents) *parents'* names?

2. What's her (brother) ____________ name?

3. What's her (husband) ____________ name?

4. What are her (children) ____________ names?

5. What are her (nephew) ____________ names?

II. Now listen and answer the questions about Ji-Hyun.

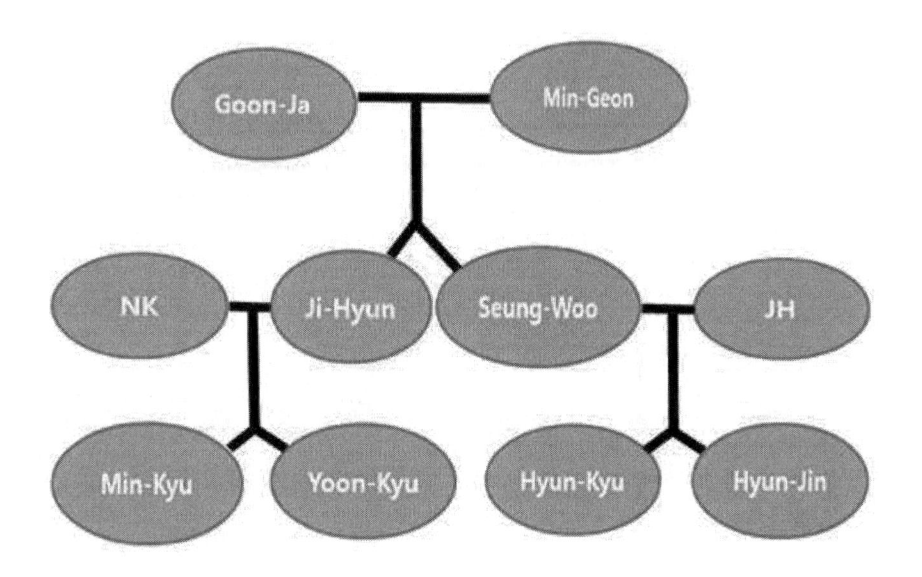

1. What are her parents names? ______________________________

2. What's her brother's name? ______________________________

3. What's her husband's name? ______________________________

4. What are her children's names? ______________________________

5. What are her nephews' names? ______________________________

Everyday Expressions!

Asking about the age

How old are you?

How old is your sister/cousin?

Are you the same age?

Is he 18?

Telling information about age

I'm 18.

She's 10.

We're both 28.

She's older. She's 12.

He's younger. He's 8.

Remember this!

Are you the same age?
→ 두 분은 (여러분은) 동갑이십니까?

We are both 28.
→ 우리 둘은 28세입니다.

아래의 두 문장에서는 'than me'이 생략되었습니다. 상대방이 나이를 누구와 비교하는지 이미 알고 있다면 'than me'를 생략할 수 있습니다.

She's older (than me).
→ 그녀는 (저보다) 나이가 많습니다.

He's younger (than me)
→ 그분은 (저보다) 어립니다.

Let's check how much you understand!

Complete the conversation using the expressions in the box.

How old are you? How old is she? How old is he How old are they? Are you the same age?

Young-Hee: **Who's that?**

Chul-Soo: **This is my wife.**

Young-Hee: **She's beautiful.** ________________________________?

Chul-Soo: **We're the same age. We're both 35.**

Young-Hee: **Really? Are those your children?**

Chul-Soo: **Yes, they are. They go to kindergarten.**

Young-Hee: ________________________________?

Chul-Soo: **Chae-Rim and Jin-Ho are the same age. They're both 5.**

Young-Hee: **Wow. Are they twins? They're beautiful.**

Chul-Soo: **Yes, they are. Thank you.**

Pronunciation

Repeat after the teacher. After that practice the conversation with the teacher.

Young-Hee: **Who's that?**

Chul-Soo: **This is my wife.**

Young-Hee: **She's beautiful. How old is she?**

Chul-Soo: **We're the same age. We're both 35.**

Young-Hee: **Really? Are those your children?**

Chul-Soo: **Yes, they are. They go to kindergarten.**

Young-Hee: **How old are they?**

Chul-Soo: **Chae-Rim and Jin-Ho are the same age.**
They're both 5.

Young-Hee: **Wow. Are they twins? They're beautiful.**

Chul-Soo: **Yes, they are. Thank you.**

Speaking

First complete the conversation with the information below. Then practice the conversation with the teacher.

You see a picture on the teacher's phone. The teacher's old student and the teacher are in the picture. You think it is a beautiful picture.

You: ______________________________
(그 사람은 누구입니까?)

Teacher: **This is my old student.**

You: ______________________________
(그녀는 몇 살 입니까?)

Teacher: **She's thirty.**

You: ______________________________
(아름다운 사진입니다.)

Teacher: **Thank you.**

Now complete the conversation with the information below. Then practice the conversation with the teacher.

The teacher and you are talking about Chul Soo's car. It's new. It's only a week old.

Teacher: **What's that?**

You: ______________________________

(철수 차입니다.)

Teacher: **Is it new?**

You: ______________________________

(맞습니다.)

Teacher: **How old is it?**

You: ______________________________

(1주일 밖에 안되었습니다.)

Teacher: Wow. It's brand new.

You: ______________________________

(맞습니다.)

What can you do now?

	Yes, I can	Mostly yes.	Not yet.
I can identify family members.			
I can talk about age.			

13 주차 1차시 학습:

Relationships

Learning Objectives:

Talk about your relationship status.

Talk about what you have.

Review

I. Complete the sentences about Ji-Hyun's family tree.

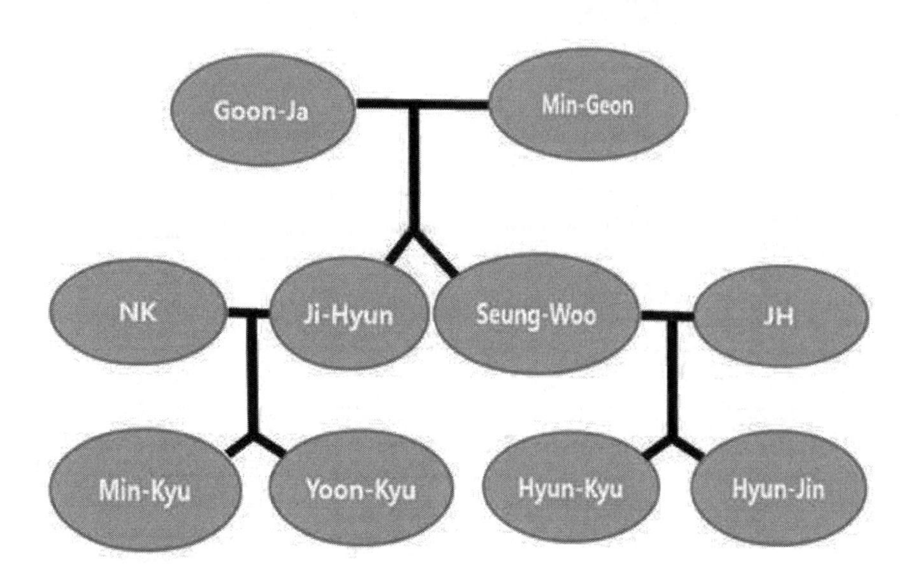

1. Ji-Hyun has nephews. She doesn't have a son/niece.

2. Hyun-Jin's father/uncle is NK.

3. Hyun-Kyu's mother/aunt is Ji-Hyun.

4. Min-Kyu and Yoon-Kyu's cousins/brothers are Hyun-Kyu and Hyun-JIn

II. Complete the questions with the possessive nouns. Use the nouns in the parentheses.

1. What's your (brother) <u>*brother's*</u> name?

2. What are your (grandparents) ______________________ names?

3. What are your (grandchildren) ______________________ names?

4. Where's the (women) ______________________ restroom?

5. Where's the (men) ______________________ restroom?

6. Are these (Min-Kyu and Yoon-Kyu) ___________________________ _______________cars?

7. Is this (Hyun-Kyu and Hyun-Jin) ______________________ car?

8. Is this (Thomas) ______________________ laptop?

III. Choose all the sentences that can be used to answer the question.

A: **How old are you?**

B: ______________________________

a. 18.
b. We're both 18.
c. We're the same age. We're both 18.
d. I'm old.

IV. Choose all the sentences that can be used to answer the question.

A: **How old is your sister?**

B: ______________________________

a. She's 18.
b. She's older. She's 18.
c. He's younger.
d. She's younger. She's 18.

Vocabulary

single	미혼의
married	결혼한
seeing someone	연애 중
a small family	핵가족
a big family	대가족
a bachelor's degree	학사학위
a good job	좋은 직장
a nice house	좋은 주택 (예쁜 주택)
a nice apartment	좋은 아파트 (예쁜 아파트)

Let's check how much you understand!

Complete the sentences using the words in the box.

single	married	seeing someone	a small family
a big family	boyfriend	girfriend	

1. I'm from ____________________ . I have a lot of sisters and brothers.

2. I'd like to have ____________________ . I plan to have just one child.

3. I'm ____________________ with two children.

4. I'm ____________________ . I have a boyfriend.

5. I'm not ____________________ . I'm seeing someone.

Remember this!

'have a family' 는 자녀를 낳고 가정을 이룬 상태를 말합니다. 그리고 요즘은 결혼은 하지 않았지만, 사귀는 사람이 있으면 미혼이 아니라고 말합니다.

Pronunciation

Repeat after the teacher.

1. I'm from a big family. I have a lot of sisters and brothers.

2. I'd like to have a small family. I plan to have just one child.

3. I'm married, and have two children.

4. I'm seeing someone. I have a boyfriend.

5. I'm not single. I'm seeing someone.

13 주차 2차시 학습:

Relationships

Learning Objectives:

Talk about your relationship status.

Talk about what you have.

Grammar

HAVE			
I	have	a sister.	I **love** her.
You			You **love** her.
We			We **love** her.
They			They **love** her.
She	has		She **loves** her.
He			He **loves** her.

HAVE			HAVE GOT		
I	have	a sister.	I	**'ve got** (have got)	a sister.
You			You		
We			We		
They			They		
She	has		She	**'s got** (has got)	
He			He		

Remember this!

'소유하다'라는 의미를 갖은 표현은 have, have got, has, has got이 있습니다.

Let's check how much you understand!

Complete the sentences with *'s got* **or** *'ve got.*

1. He ____________________ a brother.

2. They ____________________ a nice apartment.

3. She ____________________ a bachelor's degree.

4. I ____________________ a good smartphone.

5. We ____________________ a very old car, but it's still good.

Pronunciation

Repeat after the teacher.

1. He's got a brother.

2. They've got a nice apartment.

3. She's got a bachelor's degree.

4. I've got a good smartphone.

5. We've got a very old car, but it's still good.

Let's check how much you understand!

Complete the conversation using the expressions in the box.

's got	've got	How old is he?
How old is she?	How old are they?	seeing someone

Young-Hee: **Do you have a sister?**

Chul-Soo: **No, I don't. I ______________________ a brother.**

Young-Hee: **Really? ____**

Chul-Soo: **We're both 30. We're twins.**

Young-Hee: **Really? That's amazing. Is he married?**

Chul-Soo: **No, he's not. But he's ______________________ .**

Young-Hee: **That's great.**

Chul-Soo: **How about you? Do you have a sister?**

Young-Hee: **Yes, I do. Actually I ______________________ two sisters.**

Chul-Soo: ____

Young-Hee: **They're 28 and 26. They are younger.**

Pronunciation

Repeat after the teacher.

Young-Hee: **Do you have a sister?**

Chul-Soo: **No, I don't. I've got a brother.**

Young-Hee: **Really? How old is he?**

Chul-Soo: **We're both 30. We're twins.**

Young-Hee: **Really? That's amazing. Is he married?**

Chul-Soo: **No, he's not. But he's seeing someone.**

Young-Hee: **That's great.**

Chul-Soo: **How about you? Do you have a sister?**

Young-Hee: **Yes, I do. Actually I've two sisters.**

Chul-Soo: **How old are they?**

Young-Hee: **They're 28 and 26. They are younger.**

Speaking

First complete the conversation with the information below. Then practice the conversation with the teacher.

Talk about Chul-Soo's brother. Chul-Soo and his brother are twins. They're thirty. Chul-Soo's brother is seeing someone.

Teacher: **Does Chul-Soo have a brother?**

You: ______________________________

(네. 있습니다. 쌍둥이 동생이 있습니다.)

Teacher: **Really? That's amazing. How old are they?**

You: ______________________________

(둘 다 서른 살입니다.)

Teacher: **Is Chul-Soo's brother married?**

You: ______________________________

(아니요. 하지 않았습니다. 그런데 사귀는 사람이 있는 것 같습니다.)

Now complete the conversation with the information below. Then practice the conversation with the teacher.

Talk about Chul-Soo's family. He's married. He's got two children. They're twins. They're 5.

You: ____

(철수는 결혼했습니까?)

Teacher: **Yes, he is.**

You: ____

(아이가 있나요?)

Teacher: **Yes, he does. He's got two children. They're twins.**

You: ____

(아이들이 몇 살인가요?)

Teacher: **They're 5.**

You: ____

(분명 귀여울 거예요.)

Teacher: **They must be.**

What can you do now?

	Yes, I can	Mostly yes.	Not yet.
I can talk about the relationship status.			
I can talk about what I have.